…Wishing you all the best and good luck for your upcoming board examinations…

History Masterguide

Comprehensive coverage of History Syllabus, Class XII

VEDANT GUPTA

CBSE CLASS XII TOPPER (97.2%)

CBSE CLASS X Topper (99 %)

IN BHU (History Hons.)

History Masterguide by Vedant

DEDICATION

To those who seek knowledge,
to the educators who inspire curiosity,
and the historians who preserve the past
for future generations.

This work is dedicated to my family,
whose unwavering support made this journey possible,
and to my mentors,
whose guidance shaped my understanding of history.

May this book serve as a beacon for learners and educators alike.

FOREWORD

It is with great enthusiasm that I present *History Masterguide: Class 12*, a comprehensive resource designed to support students in their journey through their Class XII. This book include complete dateline, all important questions with explanations, including PYQ's, and even breakdown of complex terms.

History Masterguide has been meticulously structured to align with the Class 12 NCERT curriculum, incorporating thought-provoking questions, and a wealth of supplementary material to ensure students are well-prepared for both examinations and lifelong learning.

I extend my gratitude to my family, mentors, students and colleagues, whose encouragement and feedback have been invaluable throughout this endeavor. I also owe thanks to the educators and students whose engagement with history continues to inspire me.

Note – The explanations of last few questions of each chapter isn't made available so that you can all practice them by yourself and booast your confidence

Sincerely,
Vedant Gupta

History Hons. (BHU)

ABOUT THE AUTHOR :-

Vedant Gupta is a distinguished academic with a passion for history and education. He completed his Class X with an exceptional 99% and achieved a remarkable 97.2% in Class XII and got 200/200 in History exam of CUET demonstrating his dedication and excellence in academics. Currently pursuing a Bachelor's degree in History Honours from Banaras Hindu University (BHU), one of India's premier institutions, Vedant is committed to deepening his understanding of historical narratives and their relevance in today's world.

In addition to his academic pursuits, Vedant is an educator at an innovative online educational startup. His role involves mentoring and guiding students through Humanities subjects, emphasizing clarity, engagement, and critical thinking. With a deep commitment to fostering learning and intellectual growth, Vedant's educational philosophy is rooted in making learning accessible and inspiring for all students. Through his work, he strives to bridge the gap between traditional education and modern digital learning, shaping the future of education for the next generation

Table of Contents

Complete Time Line of History Class XII

Chapter – 1 (Bricks, Beads and Bones)

1.)	6000 – 2600 BCE	Early Harappan Culture
2.)	2600 – 1900 BCE	Mature Harappan Culture
3.)	1900 – 1300 BCE	Late Harappan Culture
4.)	By 1800 BCE	Harappan (Cholistan) - disown
5.)	1921	Harappa discovered - Dayaram Sahni
6.)	1922	Mohenjo-daro discover – RD Banerjee
7.)	1924	John Marshall announced IVC
8.)	1944	R.E.M. Wheeler - Director general ASI

Chapter-2 (Kings, Farmers and towns)

1.)	1500 – 1000 BCE	Rig Veda was Compiled
2.)	6th Cen BCE – 600 CE	Emergence of Early Kingdoms
3.)	500 – 200 BCE	Composition of Dharmasutras
4.)	1838	Decipherment of Asokan Brahmi and Kharoshti by James Princep
5.)	6th Century BCE	Turning point- early Indian history
6.)	6th – 4th Cen. BCE	Magadha Powerful mahajanapada
7.)	4th Century BCE	Magadha capital shift to Paliputra
8.)	321 BCE	Chandragupta Maurya Founded Mauryan Empire
9.)	185 BCE	End of Mauryan Empire
10.)	2nd BC - 2nd Cen CE	Satavahana Empire
11.)	1st Cen. BCE to 1st Cen. CE	Kushana Empire
12.)	320 CE	Beginning of Gupta Empire

13.)	550 CE	End of Gupta Empire
14.)	272/268 – 231 BCE	Rule of Asoka
15.)	200 – 100 BCE	~ Indo – Greek rule in Northwest ~ Cheras + Pandyas in South India
16.)	100 BCE – 200 CE	Shaka ruler in northwest
17.)	335 – 375 CE	Samudragupta rule
18.)	606 – 647 CE	Harshavardhan king of Kanauj
19.)	From 6TH Cen. BCE	Use- plough Agriculture
20.)	375 – 415 CE	Chandragupta II rule
21.)	1st Century CE	1st Gold coins- Kushana
22.)	2nd Century BCE	1st coins with name + Image - Indo greek
23.)	From 6th Cen. CE	Gold coins declined
24.)	500 – 600 CE	~ Rise of Chalukyas (Karnatakas) ~ Rise of Pallavas (Tamil Nadu)
25.)	78 CE	Kaniskha Accession
26.)	200 CE Onwards	Composition of Puranas

Chapter-3 (Kingship, Caste and Class)

1.)	500 BCE – 400 CE	Composition of Ramayana + Mahabharata
2.)	1919 – 66	Preparation + Publication of critical edition of Mahabharata
3.)	200 BCE – 200 CE	~ Manusmriti was Compiled ~ Tamil Sangam Literature
4.)	From 1000 BCE	Classification of people in Gotras
5.)	2nd Cen. CE	Rudradaman (Shaka ruler)
6.)	5th Cen. CE	Stone Inscription from Mandasor recording History of guild – silk weavers
7.)	1951 – 52	B.B. Lal excavated- village named Hastinapur

Chapter – 4 (Thinkers, Belief and Buildings)

1.) 1500 – 1000 BCE	Early vedic period
2.) 1000 – 500 BCE	Later vedic period
3.) 1818	Sanchi Stupa discover
4.) 3rd Cen. CE	Earliest Temples
5.) By 2nd Cen. BCE	Mahayana, Vaishnavism
6.) 1854	Waller Elliot visited – Amravati took Sculpture part- Madras
7.) 1796	Local Raja wanted to build temple on Ruins of Stupa at Amravati
8.) Mid 1st Mill. BCE	Major turning point- world history (Thinkers like Buddha emerged)

Chapter-5 (From the eyes of Travellers)

1.)	11th Century CE		Al – Biruni came to India

1.) 11th Century CE — Al – Biruni came to India

2.) 14th Century CE — Ibn Battuta visited India

3.) 17th Century CE — Francis Bernier – India

4.) 973 CE — Al Biruni was born

5.) 1017 CE — Mahmud invaded Khwarizm

6.) 1332 – 33 — Al – Biruni set off for India

7.) 1333 — Biruni reached Sind

8.) 1342 — Biruni proceed to china as Sultan's envoy to mongol

9.) 1347 — Biruni decided to return home to Morocco

10.) 1656 – 1668 — Bernier was in India

11.) 19th Century — Karl marx gave concept of Asiatic mode of production

Chapter – 6 (Bhakti and sufi traditions)

1.) 711 CE	Mohammad Qazim conquer Sind
2.) 13th Century CE	Establish- Delhi Sultanate
3.) 6th Century CE	Bhakti movements (Alvars, Nayanars)
4.) 9th to 13th Cen. CE	Powerful Chola ruler- south
5.) 15th – 16th Cen CE	Mirabai – woman poet
6.) 1568	Akbar gave cauldron and donation Muinuddin dargah
7.) Late 12th Cen. CE	Sufi groups migrated –India
8.) 14th Century CE	Shaikh Nizamuddin auliya
9.) 1324 – 51	Muhammad Bin Tughlaq's rule

Chapter-7 (An Imperial Capital – Vijayanagar)

1.)	1800	Colin Mackenzie visits Vijayanagar
2.)	1836	Epigraphist collecting inscription- Hampi
3.)	1856	Photographers recording Monuments- Hampi
4.)	1336	Vijayanagara empire was founded
5.)	1336 -1485	Sangama dynasty
6.)	1485 -1503	Saluvas military commanders
7.)	1529	Death of Krishnadeva Raya
8.)	By 1542	Aravidu dynasty in power
9.)	1565	Rama Raya, CM Vijayanagara led battle
10.)	15th Cent.	Abdur Razzaq visited vijayanagara
11.)	16th Cent.	Portugese traveller Barbosa
12.)	1976	Hampi - site of National Importance
13.)	1986	Hampi- World heritage by UNESCO
14.)	1512	Krishnadeva Raya acquired Raichur doab

Chapter-8 (Peasants, Zamindars and the State)

1.)	16th - 17th Cen.	85% Indian population in villages
2.)	18th Cen.	Women Zamindars in Bengal
3.)	1690	Italian traveller Giovanni Careri - India told silver travelled all around globe and reached Indi
4.)	1598	Ain - i Akbari was completed
5.)	1665	Aurangzeb instructed revenue officers Make – Annual records of no. of ryot in each village

Chapter – 9 (Colonialism and the Countryside)

1.)	1793	Permanent settlement – effect
2.)	1797	Auction in Burdwan (Bardhaman)
3.)	1770s	Rural Economy of Bengal – crisis
4.)	1930s	Great depression – Zamindars collapsed
5.)	End 18th Cen	Zamindars crisis due to revenue burden
6.)	1813	5th report submitted to British Parliament
7.)	Early 19th Cen	Buchanan travelled Rajmahal hills
8.)	1855-56	Santhal revolt
9.)	End of 1810	Buchanan cross - Ganjuria Pahar
10.)	1875	Deccan Revolt
11.)	12 May 1875	Ryots in Deccan attack shops
12.)	1818	1st revenue settlement – Bombay Deccan
13.)	1832 – 34	Famine in Deccan's countryside
14.)	1857	Cotton supply association formed Britain
15.)	1859	Manchester cotton company was formed

16.)	1859	Limitation law passed by British
17.)	1765	EIC acquires Bengal's Diwani
18.)	1773	Regulating act was passed
19.)	1861	American civil war broke out, cotton bloom
20.)	1878	Deccan Riot commission report presented to British Parliament
21.)	1800s	Santhals come to Rajmahal hills

Chapter-10 (Rebels and the Raj)

1.)	10 May 1857	Mutiny started in Meerut
2.)	11 May 1857	Sepoys at Red Fort - Bahadur Shah
3.)	23 June 1857	Centenary - Battle of Plassey
4.)	1829	Sati custom was Abolished
5.)	1851	Dalhousie described Awadh - Cheery that will drop in British mouth one day
6.)	1856	Awadh was annexed by British
7.)	1856	Summary Settlement by Brit.
8.)	1798	Subsidiary alliance introduced
9.)	1801	Subsidiary alliance imposed in Awadh
10.)	1859	~ Relief of Lucknow by Thomas Jones ~ In memoriam painted Joseph
11.)	25 Sep. 1857	James Outram and Henry Havelock in Lucknow
12.)	June 1858	Jhasi Rani got martyred

Chapter-11 (Mahatma Gandhi and the National movement)

1.)	January 1915	Gandhi returned to India
2.)	1893	Gandhi went to South Africa
3.)	1905-07	Swadeshi movement
4.)	Feb. 1916	Opening of BHU
5.)	1917	Champaran Satyagraha
6.)	1918	Ahemdabad+Kheda Satyagrah
7.)	1914-18	First world war
8.)	1919	Rowlatt act
9.)	March-April 1919	Rowlatt Satyagraha
10.)	April 1919	Jallianwala Bagh Massacre
11.)	1921	Non-Cooperation + Khilafat M.
12.)	Feb. 1922	Chauri Chaura incident
13.)	March 1922	Gandhi was arrested
14.)	Feb. 1924	Gandhi released from jail
15.)	1928	Peasant movement, Bardoli

16.)	26 Jan.1930	Independence day observed
17.)	6 April 1930	Dandi march was completed
18.)	12 March 1930	Dandi march started
19.)	1930	Civil disobedience movement
20.)	Dec. 1931	2nd Round Table Conference
21.)	March 1931	Gandhi – Irwin pact
22.)	1935	Government of India Act
23.)	8 Aug. 1942	Quit India movement
24.)	Oct. 1939	Congress ministries resigned
25.)	March 1942	Cripps mission to India
26.)	March 1940	Muslim League passes resolution autonomy of muslim areas
27.)	June 1944	Gandhi released from jail
28.)	1945	Labour gov. came in Britain
29.)	Early 1946	Fresh elections – provinces
30.)	March 1946	Cabinet mission to india

31.)	Feb. 1947	Mountbatten became Viceroy
32.)	15 Aug. 1947	Independence day India
33.)	30 Jan. 1948	Gandhi was assassinated by Godse
34.)	Dec. 1929	Congress session Lahore - Purna Swaraj

Chapter-12 (Framing the Constitution)

1.)	Dec. 1946 – Nov. 1947	Constitution of India framed
2.)	26 Jan. 1950	Republic day of India
3.)	August 1946	Great killings in Calcutta
4.)	13 Dec. 1946	Nehru introduced Objectives Resolution
5.)	1909, 1919, 1935	Government of India Act's
6.)	27 Aug. 1947	B. Pocker - demands separate electorates
7.)	12 Sep. 1947	Dhulekar's speech on Language sparked
8.)	24 Jan. 1950	~ Last meeting of Constituent assembly ~ Constitution was signed

Important Questions + PYQ's

Chapter-1 (Bricks, Beads and Bones)

1.) Highlight the role of various archaeologists in the discovery of Harappa.

2.) The most unique feature of the Harappan civilization was the development of the urban centres. Explain.

3.) Why the Harappan script is called an enigmatic script?

4.) One of the most unique features of Harappan Civilization was its carefully designed Drainage system. Elucidate.

5.) Explain the methods of irrigation used by the Harappans at different sites.

6.) What are few strategies used by archaeologist to find out social and economic differences amongst people living within a particular area?

7.) Explain how archaeologists identify the centre of craft production of the Harappan age?

8.) Explain the strategies adopted by Harappans to procure raw material for their craft production.

9.) Explain the features of Harappan Burial sites.

10.) Explain how archaeologists have been able to reconstruct diety practices of the Harappans.

11.) Write a short note on the Great Bath.

12.) Explain why seals and sealings were used by the Harappans.

13.) Mohenjo-daro was a well planned urban centre. Highlight its main features

14.) How we get to know that Harappans had contact with distant lands?

15.) Explain features of Harappan - Bricks, Seal, Weights, Beads, Script

16.) What are few evidences which suggest about the ancient authority present in Indus Valley civilization?

17.) What are the main features of the late Harappan Civilization?

18.) What might be the possible cause responsible for the end of Harappan Civilization?

19.) Explain the main problems faced by archaeologists in understanding the Harappan Civilisation.

20.) The structure of all harappan sites were divided into Two parts. Explain.

21.) Name few agricultural technologies used by the Harappans.

22.) There is evidence that by 1800 BCE most of the harappan sites had been abandoned. Substantiate the statement in the context of causes and evidence.

Chapter-2 (Kings, Farmers and towns)

1.) Explain the various sources to know about Mauryan empire.

2.) The 6th century BCE was a period of emergence of early states and empires in the early Indian history. Justify the statement.

3.) What are few limitations in Inscriptional Evidences?

4.) Explain the administrative system of Mauryan empire.

5.) Define the term Mahajanapadas. Explain their salient features.

6.) What were the different methods used by ancient kings to claim high status?

7.) Which strategies were used by countryside people from 600 BCE to 600 CE to increase their agricultural productivity?

8.) Explain the system of land grants and trade in the mahajanapadas.

9.) By Whom and how the Brahmi and kharoshti script was deciphered? Also elucidate the role of coins in decipherment of Kharoshti script?

10.) There were several developments in different parts of the subcontinent during the long span of 1500 years following the Harappan civilization. Support the statement with examples.

11.) Who was James Princep? Mention his few contributions to ancient Indian history.

12.) Point out some drawbacks/ limitations of the Mauryan empire.

13.) Explain the usage, importance and the evolution of coins in the ancient India (Kushana, Indo greeks, guptas etc.)

14.)   Were there any differences in rural society of Mahajanpadas? If so, Mention their Social division.

15.)   Point out few Contributions of Asoka in the ancient Indian history. What title he was given in inscriptions?

Chapter-3 (Kinship, Caste and Class)

1.) Mahabharata is a Dynamic text. Justify the statement.

2.) Analyse the role of scholors in the task of preparing and publishing the critical edition of Mahabharata.

3.) Historians have studied many rules and varied practices of familial ties during the Mahabharata period. Support with examples.

4.) In the ancient India, kingshipwas not only with Kshatriyas but also with non – Kshatriyas. Explain the statement with examples.

5.) In the ancient india, there was population beyond the influence of brahminical ideas of 4 Varnas. Explain the statement with examples.

6.) How was patriliny system important among the elite families from 6th century BCE onwards. Explain with examples.

7.) Why does historians analyse the familial ties and kinship during Mahabharata?

8.) Explain the excavations of B.B. Lal and his discovery of Hastinapura.

9.) What are the 2 sections in which the content of Mahabharata can be classified? Also, name the author of this text and the original language used for composition?

10.) Were there any gender differences between 600 BCE to 600 CE in land ownership and access to property? Briefly explain.

11.) Write a short note on Gotami puta Siri Satakani.

12.) Explain the basic difference between Jati and Varna.

13.) What was the right occupation described in the Dharamsutras for the 4 different Varnas?

14.) What do you mean by the term Gotra? Importance?

15.) Highlight the rules of Marriages as defined in the Dharamshastras.

16.) Difference between Endogamy and Exogamy.

17.) What- finding from critical edition- Mahabharata.

Chapter- 4 (Thinkers, beliefs and buildings)

1.)   Who was Budhha? Explain his early life and major teachings he gave?

2.)   Explain why Buddhism and Jainism grew rapidly after 5th Century BCE.

3.)   Examine the main features of Sanchi stupa and the role of rulers of Bhopal in preserving it.

4.)   Write a short note on Jainism. Elucidate the major teachings in Jainism.

5.)   Explain the growth of Puranic Hindusism. Role of philosophy and temples?

6.)   Sanchi stupa is one of the best preserved Stupa's all around India. Justify the statement.

7.)   Why is the mid 1st millennium BCE often considered as one of the major turning point in world history? Explain.

8.)   Why was Budhha considered one of the most influential teachers of his time/ explain.

9.)   Describe the notion of savior in Hinduism.

10.)   What was the sacrificial tradition in the ancient India? Describe its evolution.

11.)   Why were Buddhism and Jainism getting a lot of support and followers despite the presence of Brahminical system?

12.)   Write a short note on Buddha's Followers.

13.)   Why were stupas built in Buddhism? Highlight their importance.

14.) Define the structure of stupas.

15.) Explain the importance of H.H. Cole in preserving the Sanchi Stupa.

16.) Sanchi survived but Amravati stupa didn't. what might be the possible reason?

17.) Differentiate between Hinayana and Mahayana.

18.) Literature and texts help historians to better describe the sculptures. Justify the statement with examples.

19.) Write a short note on Shalabhanjika and Gajalakshmi (Sculptures).

Chapter-5 (From the eyes of Travellers)

1.)   What Ibn Battuta explained about system of communication in 14th Century.

2.)   Examine Battuta's views on Delhi and Daulatabad during his travel.

3.)   Examine Bernier's description of crown ownership of land and lack of private property in Mughal India.

4.)   Explain the distinctive features of Al – Biruni's Kitab-ul-Hind.

5.)   Describe in detail the experience of Ibn Battuta.

6.)   There was a difference in attitude and experience of Ibn Battuta and Francois Bernier. What were these differences?

7.)   What was Al – Biruni's thought on the Indian casteism and varna system?

8.)   What was the condition of women, sati and slave during the medieval period?

9.)   How did Bernier's description present the Indian society? Examine.

10.)   Write a detailed note on – Al – Biruni, Ibn Battuta, Francois Bernier

11.)   Examine the causes which made Al-Biruni to visit India.

12.)   Examine why Bernier called Mughal towns as camp towns.

13.)   Battuta found Delhi full of Joy and Excitement. Justify the statement

14.)   Was Bernier's description of Mughal society a Complete truth. If not, Justify with examples and references.

Chapter-6 (Bhakti and sufi traditions)

1.) Describe the teachings and philosophy of Lingayat tradition.

2.) Describe the life and contribution of Mirabai in the context of the bhakti movement in the medieval period.

3.) Describe the teachings and philosophy of kabir.

4.) Describe the teachings and philosophy of Guru Nanak Dev.

5.) Who were Alvars and Nayanars? Explain their ideas and how they establish relation with states?

6.) Who were sufi? Explain the causes of growth of Sufism and also highlight the relations of sufi with the state.

7.) Baba Guru Nanak Dev ji advocated a form of Nirguna Bhakti. Substantiate the statement.

8.) Explain the role of women devotees in the traditions of Alvars and Nayanars.

9.) Describe the teachings and philosophy of Islam.

10.) Describe the teachings and philosophy of Sufism.

11.) The alvars and nayanars initiated a bhakti movement that had support of the state. Explain.

12.) Write a short note on Shaikh Nizamuddin Auliya.

13.) What was the way by which Chishti's celebrate their devotionalism?

14.) Explain the term Khanqah. Highlight its important features.

15.) Different genres of poems and sufi poetry were growing during the bhakti and sufi movement. Substantiate the statement with examples.

16.) There was a lot of religious fermentation in North India while the southern part was witnessing some of the most popular Bhakti movements. Explain with examples.

17.) Point out one difference and one similarity between Be-Shari'a and Ba- Shari'a sufi traditions.

18.) Mention any 2 universal architectural features of Mosques.

19.) Point out one difference and one similarity between Alwars and Nayanars traditions.

20.) Why did chistis adopted local language of India during the medieval period? Explain.

Chapter-7 (An Imperial Capital – Vijayanagara)

1.) Examine the uniqueness of fortification in the Vijayanagar empire.

2.) Analyse the contribution of Colin Mackenzie towards the history of Vijayanagar.

3.) Why was the Mahanavami Dibba a centre of Vijayanagar rituals? Explain.

4.) Why was Persian ambassador Abdur Razzaq greatly impressed by fortification of Vijayanagar empire?

5.) Describe the role played by Rama Raya to bring ruin in Vijayanagara.

6.) Virupaksha temple was significant in Vijayanagara Empire. Substantiate the statement.

7.) The architecture of Vithala temple was unique. Substantiate the statement.

8.) Examine the role of Rayas and Nayakas in the Vijaynagara empire.

9.) Examine the apogee and decline of the Vijaynagara empire.

10.) Explain the distinctive features of the royal centre of Vijayanagara empire.

11.) Analyse the role of Krishnadeva Raya in the development of Vijayanagara empire.

12.) Amara Nayaka system was a major political innovation of Vijayanagara empire. Explain.

13.) What were the water resources of Vijayanagara empire?

14.) Write a detailed note on Virupaksha temple and Vitthala temple.

15.) Write a short note on -

- Lotus Mahal
- Audience hall
- Mahanavami dibba
- Hazara rama temple

16.) What was the urban core in Vijayanagara empire? What archaeological sources we have got about it?

17.) Do you think site of Vijayanagara empire was inspired by the existence of Virupaksha and pampadevi? Elucidate.

18.) What do you mean by the term Gopurams and Mandapas? Were they visible in Vijayanagara empire?

19.) Write a detailed note on Virupaksha temple and Vitthala temple.

20.) Explain the system of trade and commerce in the Vijayanagara empire.

Chapter-8 (Peasants, Zamindars and the State)

1.)   Revenue from the land was the economic mainstay of the Mughal empire. Support the statement with examples

2.)   Explain the role of Panchayats in Mughal rural society.

3.)   Explain the role played by Zamindars in the Mughal society.

4.)   Explain why were women considered as an important resource in agrarian society in 18th Century.

5.)   Ain-i-akbari is considered as a major source for the agrarian history of the 16th and 17th centuries.

6.)   What were the 2 kinds of peasants that are referred in the 17th Century sources? Explain

7.)   What were the Irrigation and agricultural technologies used in the Mughal rural society of 16th century?

8.)   Deep Inequalities existed on the basis of caste and other caste like distinctions in Mughal society. Justify with Examples.

9.)   What were Jati Panchayats in Mughal society of 16th century?

10.)   Explain the role of Village artisans in the Mughal land.

11.)   Were women important in the Mughal society. Support the statement with examples.

12.)   There were more to rural India than sedentary agriculture in the Mughal society. Justify with examples

13.)   Who were called 'Jangli' in the Mughal society, write a short note on them?

14.)   What are the different sources which highlight various arenas of 16th and 17th Century mughal society?

15.)   Write a short note on 'Ain-I Akbari'. Its Importance and content.

16.)   What are few limitations of Ain-I Akbari as highlighted by historians?

Chapter-9 (Colonialism and the Countryside)

1.) Explain the causes that led to the conflict between the Paharias of Rajmahal hills and Santhals

2.) Critically examine the Fifth report of 1813.

3.) Examine the factors that influenced the implementation of the Permanent settlement in Bengal and its Consequences.

4.) The jotedars became powerful figures in many areas of North Bengal during the end of the 18th Century. Examine the statement.

5.) Analyse how Santhals settled in the periphery of the Raj Mahal hills in the beginning of 19th Century.

6.) How did the American civil war of 1861 affect the lives of Ryots of India? Explain.

7.) Examine the causes for the failure of the zamindars to pay the revenue demand during the last decades of the 18th Century?

8.) Analyze the different aspects of the Permanent Settlement.

9.) Analyze the reasons of cotton boom in Bombay Deccan during 1830 to 1860.

10.) The Burdwan action had a strange twist and was considered a big public event in 1797. Explain the statement.

11.) Why was the permanent settlement of land revenue rarely extended beyond Bengal? Give reasons.

12.) Ryots came to see moenylenders as devious and deceitful. Examine the statement in context of the chapter Colonialism and the countryside.

13.) What was the limitation law? Why did it become as a symbol of oppression against ryots?'

14.) What revenue system was introduced in Bombay Deccan? What were its main features?

15.) Explain how the Ricardo's idea of land ownership introduced in the Bombay Deccan.

16.) Explain the impact of refusal of loans by moneylenders on the ryots? How did it impact them.

17.) Explain any 2 reasons for the failure of the Permanent settlement of the land revenue brought by British in Bengal.

18.) Explain the 2 strategies devised by the Zamindars of surviving the pressure of heavy revenue demands and possible auction of their land.

19.) Critically examine the Deccan riots commission report.

20.) Why were the big Mahals and lands of Zamindars were auctioned by the British government in 18th century?

21.) What as the Sunset law introduced by the Britishers? How was it oppressive?

Chapter-10 (Rebels and the Raj)

1.)   Why was the revolt of 1857 specially widespread in Awadh? Explain.

2.)   Why did rebel proclamations in 1857 appeal for unity to all sections of the populations? Explain.

3.)   Describe the role of art and literature in keeping alive the memory of the 1857 revolt.

4.)   Why were Britisher's so keen to acquire Awadh? Explain.

5.)   How did the rumours play an important role in moving the people to revolt against the British during 1857? Explain.

6.)   Under what circumstances did Bahadur Shah Zafar bless the rebellion of 1857? Explain.

7.)   Explain the main sources to know about the 1857 revolt.

8.)   Art and literature highlighted the importance of Lakshmi Bai. Support the statement with examples

9.)   How did the Britishers suppressed 1857 Revolt? Explain with examples.

10.) The relationship of the sepoys with the superior white officers underwent a significant change in years preceding the uprising of 1857. Justify

11.) A cherry that will drop into our mouth one day, who made this remark and explain the series of events that made the cherry to fall into the mouth of the Britishers?

12.) Examine the Subsidiary Alliance system and its provisions derived by Lord Wellesly in 1978 for India?

13.)   Write a short note on Annexation of Awadh.

14.)   Write a brief note on the following paintings/cartoons

- Relief of Lucknow
- In Memorium
- Clemency of Canning
- Justice, Punch
- Wheeler defending from sepoys

15.)   Write a short note on Annexation of Awadh.

16.)   The life was gone out of the body. What does this statement refers to? Explain.

17.)   How nationalist images plays an important role in igniting the feeling of Independence? Explain.

Chapter-11 (Mahatma Gandhi and the Nationalist Movement)

1.) Examine contribution of Gandhi towards nation after freedom.

2.) There are many different kinds of sources from which we can reconstruct the political career of Gandhi ji and the history of the Indian nationalist movement. Examine the statement.

3.) The Salt satyagraha inspired masses to participate in the CDM. Justify the statement.

4.) Mass cooperation played an important role in the success of the NCM. Justify the statement.

5.) Describe the role of Gandhi ji as a social reformer

6.) Explain the role of Gandhi ji in Civil disobedience movement.

7.) Explain the role of Gandhi ji in Non – Cooperation movement.

8.) Explain why the Quit India movement was considered a mass movement.

9.) Explain the reasons and outcomes of the salt satyagraha.

10.) Examine the causes and events of Quit India movement.

11.) As a consequence of NCM, the british raj was shaken to its foundations for the First time since the 1857 revolt. Explain the statement with exmples.

12.) Why did Gandhi choose Salt for doing the march? What does it relate to and how it became an All India campaign?

13.) Analyze Gandhi's activities in India during 1930 – 34.

14.) By 1922, Gandhi had transformed Indian nationalism. Examine the statement.

15.) Salt march was a notable event in the Indian freedom Movement. Explain with examples.

16.) What are the strengths and limitations of the sources which are used to reconstruct the political career of Mahatma Gandhi?

17.) When Gandhi returned to India in 1915, he saw many changes prevailing here. Mention any few such changes.

18.) What was the significance of Gandhi ji's speech at Banaras Hindu University?

19.) The salt march of 1930 was such a event which brought Gandhi to the world attention. Explain.

20.) Gandhiji used to give the nationalist speech in the mother tongue. What was its significance and how did he knitted the Non- Cooperation movement?

21.) Wherever Gandhi ji went, rumours of his miraculous powers spread. Examine the statement with examples.

22.) Months after Independence are often described as the finest hours of Mahatma. Justify why?

Chapter-12 (Framing the Constitution)

1.) Why did Vallabh Bhai Patel remark the British element is gone, but they have left the mischief behind?

2.) Why did some members of the constituent assembly argued for a strong centre? Explain.

3.) Explain the important role played by some members of the constituent assembly.

4.) The draft constitution provided for 3 list of subjects on the issue of federalism. Explain the statements with examples

5.) How did GB Pant show his concern in the constituent assembly for making India a unified nation? Explain.

6.) One of the topics most vigorously debated in the constituent assembly was the respective rights to the central and the state governments. Analyze the statement with supporting arguments.

7.) What was the Objective resolution? Why it is considered as a momentous resolution? Explain.

8.) Strong centre was important. What were the arguments in support of it?

9.) Linguistic issues were hotly debated in Constituent assembly. Justify statement with examples

10.) Who were the main supporters and opponents of separate electorate in India for religious minority and what they argue for it

11.) Mention arguments given by Balakrishna Sharma for greater power to centre?

12.) Describe the different arguments made in favor of protection of depressed class in the constituent assembly.

13.) The discussions in constituent assembly were also influenced by the public opinions. Support the statement

14.) A communist member Somnath Lahri saw the dark hands of Britishers hanging over the deliberations of constituent assembly. Examine the statement.

15.) How did power of Central govt. protected by the Constituent assembly. Explain.

16.) What was the opinion of Ambedkar regarding the protection of Depressed caste?

17.) RV Dhulekar's speech resulted in a tussle over language issue and was fiery, hurting linguistic sentiments. Examine

18.) What was the demand made by B. Pocker Bahadur? Was it accepted or opposed Explain briefly?

Important Terms – History

1.)	Piyadassi	Pleasant to behold, refers to Asoka
2.)	Dhamma	Teachings of Buddha
3.)	Dhamma – Mahamatta	Special officers appointed by Asoka to spread message of Dhamma
4.)	Chief	Powerful man whose power may or may not be hereditary
5.)	Devaputra	Son of God, title of Kushana rulers
6.)	Prashastis	Poem in praise of kings
7.)	Samantas	Men who maintained themselves resources
8.)	Gahapatis	Owner/master of a household
9.)	Vellalar	Large landowners
10.)	Uzhavar	Ploughmen
11.)	Adimai	Slaves
12.)	Successful Merchants	Masattuvans (tamil, setthis), satthavahas- Prakrit
13.)	Devanampiya	Beloved of gods, Refers – Asoka
14.)	Kula	Designate Families

15.)	Jnati	Larger network of kinfolk
16.)	Vamsha	Lineage
17.)	Patriliny	Descent from father to son, so on
18.)	Matriliny	Descent is traced from Mother
19.)	Endogamy	marriage within a unit, caste, group
20.)	Exogamy	marriage outside unit, caste, group
21.)	Polygyny	Practice of man having several wives
22.)	Polyandry	Women having several husbands
23.)	Dharmasutras	Sanskrit texts containing norms
24.)	Gotras	descendants in an unbroken chain
25.)	Metronymics	Names derived from mother
26.)	Varnas	4 Categories
27.)	Mlechchhas	Refers Shakas, outsiders
28.)	Nishadas	People living in the forests
29.)	Suvarnakara	Goldsmiths
30.)	Chandalas	people dealing with disposal of corpes
31.)	Didactic	meant for purpose of instuctions

32.)	Kutagrahashala	Hut with pointed roof
33.)	Tirthankaras	those who guide men or women across the river of existence
34.)	Hagiography	Biography of a saint leader
35.)	Anicca	Transient
36.)	Anatta	Soulless
37.)	Nibbana	extinguishing ego and desire
38.)	Sangha	organization of monks
39.)	Bhikkhus	people who live on alms
40.)	Metta	fellow feeling
41.)	Karuna	compassion
42.)	Chaityas	sites with small shrine attached
43.)	Harmika	balcony like structure, home of god
44.)	Yashti	Mast above harmika
45.)	Mahaparinibbana	State entered after nirvana
46.)	Shalabhanjika	Women whose touch cause trees to Flower and bear fruit
47.)	Theravadas	Path of old, respected teachers

48.)	Hinayana	Lesser vehicle
49.)	Mahanaya	Greater vehicle
50.)	Garbhagriha	Small square room for God
51.)	Metrology	science of measurement
52.)	Qazi	Judge
53.)	Antyaja	People born outside caste system
54.)	Saguna	Bhakti with attributes
55.)	Nirguna	Bhakti without attributes
56.)	Alvars	Devotion of Vishnu
57.)	Nayanars	Devotion of Shiva
58.)	Virashaivas	Heroes of Shiva
59.)	Lingayats	weavers of the lingas
60.)	Jangama	wandering monks
61.)	Ulama	Scholars of Islamic studies
62.)	Shari'a	Law governing muslim community
63.)	Zimmi	Protected people
64.)	Jizya	Zimmi paid a tax and gained right To be protected by muslim rulers

65.)	Shahada	Messenger i.e. here Prophet Muhammad
66.)	Namaz / Salat	Prayers 5 times a day by muslims
67.)	Sawm	fasting during Ramzan month
68.)	Hajj	pilgrimage to Mecca
69.)	Khojahs	branch of Ismailis (shi'a sect)
70.)	Ginan	derived from Sanskrit jnana - knowledge
71.)	Minbar	Pulpit
72.)	Turushka	Turkish rulers
73.)	Tajika	People from Tajikistan
74.)	Parashika	People from Persia
75.)	Khanqah	Hospice/ abode for the sufi's
76.)	Shaikh, pir, murshid	Teaching master in the khanqah
77.)	Murids	Disciples of sheikh
78.)	Khalifa	Successor or the next master
79.)	Silsila	Chain signifying continuous link between master-disciple stretching unbroken
80.)	Dargah	Tomb Shrine of a Shaikh (court)

81.)	Ziyarat	Pilgrimage to dargah
82.)	Wali	cult of the Shaikh
83.)	Tasawwuf	Sufism
84.)	Be – Shari'a	Who were not bound by Islamic laws
85.)	Ba – Shari'a	Those who follow the Islamic laws
86.)	Jama'at Khana	Big hall where inmates lived, prayed
87.)	Langar	Open Kitchen for food charity
88.)	Futuh	Unasked for charity
89.)	Qawwals	specially trained musicians perform mystical chants
90.)	Zikr	Reciting the God's name
91.)	Sama	Performance of mystical music
92.)	Masnavis	Long poems to express divine love using human love as an allegory
93.)	Auqaf	Charitable trusts
94.)	Sultan – ul - Mashaikh	Sultan among Shaikhs, refers to Nizamuddin
95.)	Ulatbansi	upside – down sayings
96.)	Julahas	Community of weavers

97.)	Shabad	Hymns
98.)	Khalsa Panth	Army of the Pure
99.)	Sangat	Rules for congregational worship
100.)	Rab	Absolute God
101.)	Nam – Simaran	Remembrance of God's name
102.)	Alakh	the unseen
103.)	Nirakar	formless
104.)	Shunya	emptiness
105.)	Shabda	sound
106.)	Vijaynagara	City of Victory, Karnataka samrajyamu
107.)	Gajapatis	Lord of Elephants
108.)	Rayas	Kings in Vijayanagara
109.)	Nayakas	Military chiefs in Vijayanagara
110.)	Amara - Nayakas	Military commanders, given territory to govern by Rayas
111.)	Hindu Suratrana	Hindu Sultans
112.)	Gopurams	Royal Gateways
113.)	Mandapas	Pavilions

114.)	**Raiyat**	Peasants/ Kisan/ asami
115.)	**Khud – kashta**	Peasants who are residents of village in which they own land
116.)	**Pahi – kashta**	Non – resident cultivators who beloned to other village
117.)	**Jins – I – kamil**	perfect / high revenue crops
118.)	**Muqaddam**	Villagwe Headmen/ Mandal
119.)	**Majur**	Agricultural labourers
120.)	**Halalkhorans**	Scavengers
121.)	**Mallahzadas**	sons of boatmen
122.)	**Miras/ Watan**	Hereditary land
123.)	**Mawas**	a place of refugees
124.)	**Pargana**	administrative subdivision of Mughal
125.)	**Peshkash**	Tribute collected by Mughals
126.)	**Pirs**	Sufi saints
127.)	**Khidmat**	certain services
128.)	**Milkiyat**	personal land of Zamindars
129.)	**Qilachas**	Fortresses owned by Zamindars

130.)	Sanad	Imperial order
131.)	Amil – Guzar	Revenue Collector
132.)	Jama	Amount assessed
133.)	Hasil	Amount collected
134.)	Manzil – Abadi	concerns imperial house
135.)	Sipah – Abadi	military affairs
136.)	Mansabdars	Imperial officers
137.)	Measured area	Zamin- i –paimuda
138.)	Naqdi	revenue assessed in cash
139.)	Suyurghal	Revenue grants in charity
140.)	Sawar	Horsemen
141.)	Piyada	Foot – soldiers
142.)	Fil	Elephants
143.)	Tulaqdar	one who holds a tulaq
144.)	Ryots	designate Peasants
145.)	Amlah	officer of Zamindar
146.)	Adhiyars/bargadars	Sharecroppers

147.) Jotedars	Mandal, gantidar, haoladar
148.) Dikus	Moneylenders
149.) Rentier	people who live on rent
150.) Sahukar	Moneylender + Trader
151.) Lathyal	having lathi −Strongmen of Zamindar

Explanation of All Important Questions

Chapter – 1 (Bricks, Beads and Bones)

Ans - 1.) Any Other Similar Points to be evaluated

- **Alexander Cunningham (Mid-19th Century)**

  - Focused on Early Historic archaeology using texts and inscriptions as guides.

- **Daya Ram Sahni (1920s)**

  - Discovered seals at Harappa in older layers, marking a pre-Early Historic era.

- **Rakhal Das Banerji (1920s)**

  - Found similar seals at Mohenjodaro, linking sites to a unified culture.

- **John Marshall (1924)**

  - Announced the discovery of the Indus Valley Civilization, contemporaneous with Mesopotamia.

- **John Marshall's Contribution**

  - Introduced professional archaeology in India, focusing on everyday life patterns.

- **R.E.M. Wheeler (1944)**

  - Revolutionized excavation methods by emphasizing stratigraphy over uniform digging.

- **S.N. Roy's Observation**

  The Story of Indian Archaeology, "Marshall left India three thousand years older than he had found her."

Ans - 2.) Any Other Similar Points to be evaluated

- **City Layout**

    - Harappan cities were divided into two parts: the Citadel (for administrative and ceremonial activities) and the Lower Town (for residential and commercial use).

- **Grid Pattern**

    - Streets were laid out in a grid pattern, with main roads cutting at right angles, showcasing advanced town planning.

- **Drainage System**

    - The cities had a well-organized drainage system with covered drains, inspection holes, and slope designs to prevent waterlogging.

- **Standardized Bricks**

    - Burnt bricks of uniform size were used for construction, reflecting a standardized approach across settlements.

- **Public Buildings**

    - Structures like the Great Bath in Mohenjo-daro and granaries in Harappa indicate centralized planning for community activities and storage.

- **Residential Architecture**

    - Houses were built with multiple rooms, bathrooms, and private wells, indicating concern for hygiene and comfort.

- **Specialized Areas**

    - Separate areas for craft production and storage of goods suggest economic and functional zoning.

- **Integration of Public and Private Spaces**

    - The seamless blend of public infrastructure with private housing indicates effective civic planning – Great Bath, Granary, etc

Ans – 3.) Any Other Similar Points to be evaluated

The Harappan script is called an enigmatic script because it has not been deciphered –

1.) Lack of Bilingual Texts: No bilingual inscriptions have been found

2.) Unresolved Symbolism: The symbols used in the script do not correlate with known languages or other ancient scripts

3.) Short Inscriptions: Most inscriptions are very brief, limiting the ability to understand context or grammatical structure

4.) Limited Number of Symbols: The script consists of around 400-600 symbols, and their meanings remain speculative

5.) Absence of Context: Harappan script appears mostly on seals and tablets, without sufficient context to interpret its use.

These factors contribute to the script being a mystery in the study of the Harappan Civilization.

Ans – 4.) Any Other Similar Points to be evaluated

- **Well-Planned Layout**: Harappan cities had a grid pattern with drains running alongside streets.

- **Covered Drains**: Drains were covered with slabs or bricks for sanitation.

- **Interconnected System**: Houses were connected to street drains through smaller channels.

- **Manholes for Maintenance**: Drains had manholes for regular cleaning and maintenance.

- **Wastewater Management**: Wastewater from houses was directed into soak pits or street drains.

- **Uniform Design**: Drainage systems were standardized across different Harappan cities.

- **Engineering Precision**: The gradient ensured water flowed smoothly without stagnation.

- **Emphasis on Hygiene**: The advanced drainage system reflects the importance of public health

Ans - 5.) Any Other Similar Points to be evaluated

- **Canals**: Evidence of canal irrigation has been found at sites like Shortughai in Afghanistan.

- **Wells**: Wells were a common feature in Harappan settlements for drawing water.

- **Reservoirs**: At Dholavira, large reservoirs were constructed to store rainwater.

- **Check Dams**: Stone bunds or dams were used to control water flow and conserve water at Dholavira.

- **Floodwater Utilization**: Harappans used floodwaters of rivers like the Indus for irrigation.

- **Tank Irrigation**: Rainwater harvesting was practiced through tanks and storage pits.

- **Field Channels**: Fields were irrigated using simple channels to divert water from natural sources.

- **Adaptation to Terrain**: Irrigation methods varied depending on geographical conditions of the site.

Ans-6.) Any Other Similar Points to be evaluated

- **Burial Pit Variations**: Differences in burial pits, such as brick-lined spaces, may indicate social differences.

- **Grave Goods**: Items like pottery, ornaments, and copper mirrors in burials suggest varying beliefs and status.

- **Gender-Neutral Jewellery**: Jewellery found with both men and women indicates shared access to ornaments.

- **Rare Burial Finds**: Unique ornaments like shell rings and jasper beads hint at wealth or status.

- **Utilitarian Artefacts**: Common items like querns, pottery, and needles reflect daily use and wide distribution.

- **Luxury Artefacts**: Rare or non-local materials like faience or intricate technologies denote elite possession.

- **Material Analysis**: Use of costly or imported materials like semi-precious stones indicates wealth.

- **Craft Complexity**: Items requiring advanced techniques, such as faience pots, suggest luxury

Ans – 7.) Any Other Similar Points to be evaluated

- **Abundance of Waste Materials**: Sites with large quantities of waste like stone chips and unfinished objects indicate craft production.

- **Specialized Workshops**: Presence of areas dedicated to crafting, such as bead-making workshops.

- **Tools and Equipment**: Discovery of tools like drills, furnaces, and molds used for crafting.

- **Raw Material Sources**: Proximity to raw material sources like stones, shells, or metals.

- **Finished and Unfinished Goods**: Sites with both finished and unfinished products

- **Standardized Artefacts**: Consistency in design and production techniques points to centralized manufacturing.

- **Distribution Networks**: Evidence of crafted items being distributed to other sites

- **Craft Debris**: Large quantities of craft-related debris, such as faience or terracotta fragments, signal production activities.

Ans – 8.) Any Other Similar Points to be evaluated

- **Local Resources**: Used locally available materials like clay for pottery and mud bricks.

- **Long-Distance Trade**: Traded with distant regions for rare materials like lapis lazuli from Afghanistan and copper from Rajasthan.

- **Direct Procurement**: Sent expeditions to resource-rich areas, like Khetri for copper and Gujarat for semi-precious stones.

- **Trade Networks**: Maintained trade links with Mesopotamia, Oman, and Bahrain for items like tin and shell.

- **Exchange Systems**: Bartered finished goods like beads and seals for raw materials.

- **Coastal Collection**: Harvested shells from coastal areas like Nageshwar and Balakot.

- **Caravan Routes**: Used overland caravan routes for transporting goods from distant regions.

- **Riverine Transport**: Utilized rivers for moving bulk raw materials efficiently.

Ans - 9.) Any Other Similar Points to be evaluated

- **Terracotta Figurines**: Found female figurines, possibly representing a mother goddess.

- **Seals with Religious Motifs**: Seals depicting animals and deities, like the "Proto-Shiva" figure in a yogic posture.

- **Animal Symbols**: Reverence for animals like the bull, evident in seals and figurines.

- **Sacred Trees**: Depictions of trees on seals, indicating their religious significance.

- **Phallic Symbols**: Discovery of objects resembling lingas suggests fertility worship.

- **Fire Altars**: Structures at sites like Kalibangan may indicate ritual practices involving fire.

- **Water Worship**: Presence of the Great Bath at Mohenjo-Daro points to ritual bathing practices.

- **Burial Practices**: Grave goods and burial styles suggest beliefs in an afterlife

Ans – 10.) Any Other Similar Points to be evaluated

- **Simple Pits**: The dead were usually buried in simple rectangular or oval pits.

- **Brick-Lined Graves**: Some burials had hollowed-out spaces lined with bricks.

- **Grave Goods**: Items like pottery, ornaments, and tools were often buried with the dead.

- **Ornaments for Both Genders**: Jewellery was found in the burials of both men and women.

- **Secondary Burials**: Evidence of burials without skeletons, possibly for symbolic purposes.

- **Multiple Types**: Variations include extended burials (full skeleton) and pot burials (remains in pots).

- **Cemetery Sites**: Large burial grounds like Cemetery R in Harappa indicate organized burial practices.

- **Minimal Precious Items**: Few precious objects were buried, suggesting limited belief in material offerings for the afterlife.

Ans - 11.) Any Other Similar Points to be evaluated

- **Location**: The Great Bath is located in Mohenjo-Daro, one of the prominent Harappan cities.

- **Structure**: It is a large rectangular tank made of baked bricks with watertight plaster.

- **Design**: Surrounded by colonnades and rooms, possibly for changing or rituals.

- **Staircases**: Steps on both ends lead into the tank for easy access.

- **Water Management**: Equipped with an efficient drainage system for water inflow and outflow.

- **Purpose**: Likely used for ritual bathing or religious ceremonies.

- **Waterproofing**: The floor was coated with bitumen for waterproofing.

- **Significance**: Reflects advanced engineering and the importance of water in Harappan culture.

Ans -12.) Any Other Similar Points to be evaluated

- **Identity Markers**: Seals were used to denote the identity of individuals or groups.

- **Trade Authentication**: Sealings were used to secure goods during trade and confirm authenticity.

- **Administrative Control**: Helped in managing and organizing trade and transactions.

- **Ownership Indication**: Seals indicated ownership of goods or property.

- **Symbolic Value**: Often featured religious or symbolic motifs, reflecting cultural beliefs.

- **Communication Tool**: Seals with inscriptions may have conveyed specific messages.

- **Widespread Usage**: Found variety of materials, including clay, metal, - diverse functions

- **Decorative Element**: Some seals may have been used as ornaments or amulets.

Ans - 13.) Any Other Similar Points to be evaluated

- **Grid Layout**: Mohenjo-Daro had a well-planned grid pattern of streets, intersecting at right angles.

- **Drainage System**: The city featured an advanced, covered drainage system to ensure sanitation.

- **Residential Areas**: Houses were made of baked bricks, with flat roofs and private wells.

- **Citadel and Lower Town**: The city was divided into two sections: the citadel (for elite) and lower town (for commoners).

- **Public Buildings**: Notable structures like the Great Bath and large granaries were centrally located.

- **Water Supply**: Private wells and public baths provided access to water.

- **Standardized Brick Size**: Uniform brick size used in construction, indicating central planning.

- **Economic Organization**: Evidence of organized economic activities, - craft production and trade.

Ans - 14.) Any Other Similar Points to be evaluated

- **Imported Materials**: Harappans imported materials like lapis lazuli from Afghanistan and copper from Oman.

- **Seals and Sealings**: Harappan seals have been found in Mesopotamia, indicating trade relations.

- **Beads and Artifacts**: Harappan beads and pottery have been discovered in distant regions like Mesopotamia and Bahrain.

- **Trade Items**: Items such as ivory and carnelian from Harappa were exchanged with distant lands.

- **Cultural Similarities**: Similar motifs and designs on Harappan seals and Mesopotamian art suggest cultural interaction.

- **Maritime Routes**: Evidence of maritime trade routes connecting the Indus Valley with regions like Oman and Persia.

Ans – 15.) Any Other Similar Points to be evaluated

- **Bricks**: Harappans used standardized, baked bricks of uniform size for construction, reflecting advanced urban planning.

- **Seals**: Made of steatite, Harappan seals were inscribed with animal motifs and possibly used for trade, administration, or religious purposes.

- **Weights**: The Harappans used cubical and cylindrical weights made of stone, indicating a standardized system for trade and measurement.

- **Beads**: Beads of various materials like semi-precious stones, glass, and clay were produced in workshops, indicating craft specialization and trade.

- **Script**: The Harappan script, found on seals and pottery, remains undeciphered and consists of symbols that likely served administrative or trade functions.

Ans – 16.) Any Other Similar Points to be evaluated

- **Standardized Weights and Measures**: The use of uniform weights and measures across Harappan sites suggests a central authority overseeing trade and commerce.

- **Urban Planning**: The grid-like city layouts, drainage systems, and public buildings like granaries indicate organized governance and urban management.

- **Seals and Sealings**: Seals with symbols and inscriptions suggest administrative control, likely used for trade and marking ownership.

- **Centralized Storage**: Granaries and other storage facilities found at sites like Mohenjo-Daro indicate central control over food and resources.

- **Architectural Uniformity**: The consistent use of standardized construction materials, like uniform bricks, points to centralized planning and authority.

- **Burial Practices**: Differences in burial practices, with elaborate burials for some, suggest a hierarchical society possibly governed by a ruling elite.

Ans - 17.) Any Other Similar Points to be evaluated

- **Decline of Urban Planning**: The systematic urban layout and advanced drainage systems seen in the Mature Harappan phase were largely abandoned.

- **Decentralized Settlements**: The rise of smaller, less organized settlements, often lacking the sophisticated infrastructure of earlier cities.

- **Change in Pottery**: A shift to new pottery styles, such as painted grey ware, which replaced the earlier red and black pottery.

- **Less Intensive Trade**: Decline in long-distance trade, particularly with Mesopotamia, and a reduced use of Harappan seals.

- **Agricultural Shifts**: Evidence of changes in agricultural practices, including the decline in the cultivation of certain crops.

- **Emergence of New Cultural Practices**: New forms of material culture, like the increased use of coarse pottery and the appearance of different tools and weapons.

- **Decline in Craft Production**: A reduction in specialized craft production, including bead-making and metalworking.

- **Possible Environmental Factors**: Evidence suggesting climate change and river course shifts as potential factors contributing to the civilization's decline.

Note – The Remaining questions are for your practice, hence their solutions aren't provided, Keep Practicing..!

Chapter – 2 (Kings, Farmers and Towns)

Ans – 1.) Any Other Similar Points to be evaluated

- **Inscriptions**: The edicts of Ashoka, including Rock and Pillar Edicts, provide insights into the Mauryan administration, policies, and social values.

- **Archaeological Evidence**: Excavations at sites like Pataliputra, Taxila, and Patliputra reveal urban planning, public buildings, and artifacts.

- **Literary Sources**: Texts like *Arthashastra* by Kautilya and *Indica* by Megasthenes offer detailed accounts of the political and administrative structure.

- **Coins**: Mauryan coins, often inscribed with royal symbols, provide information about the economy and royal authority.

- **Foreign Accounts**: Accounts by Greek historians and ambassadors like Megasthenes give external perspectives on Mauryan society and governance.

Ans – 2.) Any Other Similar Points to be evaluated

- **Rise of Mahajanapadas**: Around this time, the 16 Mahajanapadas (large kingdoms or republics) emerged, replacing tribal republics and marking the beginning of more centralized political structures.

- **Economic Growth**: Increased agricultural productivity, trade, and urbanization led to the accumulation of wealth, which helped in the formation of powerful states.

- **Political Consolidation**: Powerful kingdoms like Magadha, Kosala, and Kashi consolidated political control over larger regions, setting the stage for the formation of empires.

- **Religious and Philosophical Changes**: The period saw the rise of Jainism and Buddhism, which challenged traditional social structures and contributed to the intellectual and cultural development of early states.

- **Military and Administrative Systems**: The development of organized armies, administrative systems, and urban planning in cities like Pataliputra reflected the growing complexity of governance during this time.

Ans - 3.) Any Other Similar Points to be evaluated

- **Geographical Limitations**: Inscriptions are often found in specific regions, and many areas remain unexplored, limiting their representativeness of the entire empire or civilization.

- **Fragmentary Nature**: Many inscriptions are incomplete or damaged, making it difficult to fully understand the context or message.

- **Bias in Content**: Inscriptions often reflect the perspective of the ruling class or elite, and may omit critical details about the lives of common people or less favorable events.

- **Language Barriers**: The language or script used in inscriptions may be difficult to decipher, and in some cases, it remains undecoded.

- **Lack of Context**: Inscriptions, especially on stone or metal, may not provide enough context for understanding the broader social, economic, or cultural conditions of the time.

- **Limited Scope**: They often focus on royal decrees, religious matters, or political affairs, and do not offer a comprehensive view of daily life, trade, or local issues.

Ans - 4.)

- **Centralized Government**: The Mauryan Empire had a highly centralized administration, with the emperor at the top, exercising control over the entire empire.

- **Bureaucracy**: The empire was governed by a well-organized bureaucracy, with officials handling different administrative functions, including taxation, law enforcement, and military affairs.

- **Provinces**: The empire was divided into provinces, each governed by a royal prince or an appointed official. Provinces were further divided into districts for local administration.

- **Officials and Officers**: Key officers included the *Samaharta* (tax collector), *Dandapati* (chief of law and order), and *Pradeshika* (governor of a province), who helped manage various aspects of governance.

- **Army and Police**: The state maintained a strong military and a police force for maintaining law and order. Ashoka's inscriptions mention the importance of justice and policing.

- **Trade and Economy**: The government played a significant role in regulating trade, markets, and industries, and was involved in state-controlled production, such as mining and textiles.

- **Council of Ministers**: The emperor was advised by a council of ministers, as indicated in Kautilya's *Arthashastra*, which provides insights into the Mauryan political and administrative system.

- **Sub committees** - Megasthenes mentions a committee with six subcommittees for coordinating military activity, the navy, the second managed transport and provisions, foot-soldiers, horses, the fifth for chariots and the sixth for elephants.

Ans-5.)

Mahajanapadas - were 16 large, powerful kingdoms or republics that existed in ancient India around the 6th century BCE.

Salient Features:

- **Political Structure**: Included both monarchies and republics with centralized or collective rule.

- **Territorial Expansion**: Located in fertile regions with some fortified capitals for defense.

- **Agricultural Economy**: Depended on advanced agriculture, supported by irrigation and trade.

- **Urbanization**: Developed major towns and cities as administrative, cultural, and trade centers.

- **Military Strength**: Maintained strong armies for defense and territorial expansion.

- **Religious Influence**: Patronized Vedic rituals, and saw the rise of Buddhism and Jainism.

- **Trade and Craft**: Engaged in local and long-distance trade, promoting craft industries.

Ans-6.)

- **Royal Titles**: Kings adopted grand titles like *Piyadassi or Devanampiya or Devaputra by Kushanas* to signify their authority.

- **Religious Patronage**: They supported religious rituals and institutions to legitimize their rule.

- **Monuments and Inscriptions**: Kings erected monuments and issued inscriptions to glorify their achievements.

- **Warfare and Conquests**: Military victories were used to demonstrate power and expand territory.

- **Wealth and Gifts**: Kings showcased their wealth through lavish court ceremonies, gifts, and donations to temples.

Ans-7.)

- **Irrigation Systems**: Development of wells, canals, and reservoirs to ensure water supply for crops.

- **Crop Rotation**: Practicing crop rotation to maintain soil fertility and improve yields.

- **Use of Iron Tools**: Introduction of iron ploughs and other tools for more efficient farming.

- **Land Clearing**: Clearing forests and expanding cultivable land for agriculture.

- **Terracing**: Creating terraces on hilly areas to prevent soil erosion and enhance farming.

- **Improved Seeds**: Use of better-quality seeds and new farming techniques to increase crop yields.

Ans-8.)

Land Grants:

- **Royal Patronage**: Kings granted land to priests, soldiers, and sometimes to local administrators as rewards for services rendered.

- **Tax Exemption**: Land granted to religious institutions or individuals often came with tax exemptions to ensure their economic viability.

- **Agricultural Development**: Land grants were also given to encourage agricultural expansion, with the expectation of increased agricultural production and revenue.

Trade:

- **Internal Trade**: Trade flourished within Mahajanapadas, with agricultural produce, crafts, and textiles being exchanged in local markets and towns.

- **External Trade**: Long-distance trade links were established with Central Asia, Southeast Asia, and the Mediterranean. Goods like spices, silk, and precious metals were traded.

- **Urban Centers**: Towns like Pataliputra and Taxila became key commercial hubs, promoting trade through markets and organized networks.

- **Coinage**: Coins were used as a medium of exchange, facilitating both local and long-distance trade.

Ans- 9.)

- **Brahmi Script**:

    - Deciphered by **James Prinsep** in 1837 by studying inscriptions, particularly those of Ashoka, and comparing them with known languages.

- **Kharosthi Script**:

    - Deciphered by **James Prinsep** by analyzing inscriptions in the Gandhara region, comparing them with Greek and Aramaic scripts.

- **Role of Coins in Decipherment of Kharosthi**:

    - Coins issued by Greek and Indo-Greek rulers featured inscriptions in both Greek and Kharosthi, helping Prinsep establish correspondences between the two scripts.

Ans-10.)

- **Rise of Mahajanapadas** (6th century BCE): Powerful kingdoms and republics like Magadha, Kosala, and Vajjis emerged, leading to political and economic advancements.

- **Vedic Period** (1500–500 BCE): The composition of the Vedas and the establishment of the varna system marked the cultural and social development in early Indian society.

- **Urbanization** (6th–5th century BCE): The rise of cities such as Pataliputra, Vaishali, and Ujjain as trade and political centers.

- **Buddhism and Jainism** (6th century BCE): The emergence of new religious movements that influenced social and cultural practices.

- **Mauryan Empire** (c. 322–185 BCE): The rise of a centralized, vast empire under Chandragupta Maurya and Ashoka, promoting administration, trade, and cultural diffusion.

- **Post-Mauryan Period** (after 185 BCE): The development of regional powers like the Shungas, Kushanas, and Satavahanas, contributing to political and cultural diversification.

Note – The Remaining questions are for your practice, hence their solutions aren't provided, Keep Practicing..!

Chapter - 3 (Kinship, Caste and Class)

Ans - 1.)

- **Multiple Versions**: The Mahabharata exists in several versions across different regions, with varying narratives and interpretations.

- **Evolving Story**: Over centuries, new stories, characters, and elements were added to the original text.

- **Diverse Themes**: The text includes a variety of themes like dharma, ethics, politics, and war, making it adaptable to different social contexts.

- **Incorporation of Local Legends**: Local stories and legends were incorporated into the Mahabharata, reflecting the cultural diversity of ancient India.

- **Philosophical Interpretations**: The text has been interpreted in various philosophical ways, from religious to political viewpoints.

- **Influence on Other Texts**: The Mahabharata inspired other literary and religious works, influencing later texts like the *Ramayana* and Buddhist scriptures.

- **Cultural and Religious Role**: It played a significant role in shaping Hindu cultural and religious practices, adapting over time.

- **Oral Tradition**: The Mahabharata was passed down orally before being written down, allowing for its continuous transformation and adaptation across generations

Ans- 2.)

- **Textual Comparison**: Scholars compared various manuscripts of the *Mahabharata* from different regions to identify differences and similarities.

- **Elimination of Later Additions**: Scholars worked to distinguish original verses from later interpolations and additions.

- **Critical Analysis**: They critically analyzed the text to create a coherent and authentic version, removing inconsistencies.

- **Incorporating Regional Variants**: Scholars included regional versions, maintaining the diversity of narratives while ensuring textual accuracy.

- **Language and Translation**: They translated the text into different languages, making it accessible to a wider audience.

- **Preserving Tradition**: Scholars preserved the cultural and historical significance of the *Mahabharata*, while modernizing its accessibility for contemporary readers.

- **Collaborative Effort**: The task was a collaborative effort involving scholars, linguists, and historians, ensuring a comprehensive approach to the critical edition

Ans-3.)

- **Marriage Alliances**: Marriage was often used to form political alliances, such as Draupadi's marriage to the Pandavas, which linked them with various kingdoms.

- **Inheritance**: The Mahabharata highlights the importance of inheritance, seen in the dispute over the throne of Hastinapura between the Kauravas and Pandavas, showcasing the significance of succession and family rights.

- **Role of Women**: The text portrays the roles of women in the family, such as Kunti and Draupadi, who had influential roles within their familial and political spheres, despite the patriarchal structure.

- **Brotherhood and Kinship**: The *Mahabharata* emphasizes the concept of *brotherhood* and *kinship*, as seen in the relationship between the Pandavas, who shared a common bond, and in the complex dynamics between the Kauravas and Pandavas.

- **Disinheritance and Exile**: The episode of the disinheritance of Yudhishthira and the Pandavas' subsequent exile reflects the practice of how family disputes and power struggles could lead to dramatic outcomes, including loss of inheritance and status.

- **Patriarchal Authority**: The text also highlights the authority of elders, such as Bhishma, who upholds the family's honor and legacy, reinforcing patriarchal norms in decision-making within the family.

- **Role of Fosterage**: Instances like Karna's fosterage by Adhiratha and his rise in status as a Kshatriya illustrate the fluidity in family ties and kinship outside biological relationships

Ans – 4.) • **Mauryan Empire**: Chandragupta Maurya, the founder of the Mauryan Empire, was from a non-Kshatriya background, highlighting the rise of non-Kshatriyas to power.

- **Magadha Kingdom**: The rise of the Magadha kingdom under rulers like Bimbisara and Ajatashatru, who were from non-Kshatriya backgrounds, demonstrates the political ascent of non-Kshatriyas.

- **Shudra Kings**: Some Shudra-origin kings - Satavahana dynasty, ruled significant parts of India.

- **Brahmin Kings**: Kings like the Kushana rulers (e.g., Kanishka), who were from non-Kshatriya or mixed backgrounds, also exercised royal authority

Ans-5.)

- **Indigenous Groups**: Tribal communities, such as the *Mlechchhas*, *Vratyas*, and *Dasa*, were often outside the traditional Varna system and had their own social structures, customs, and beliefs.

- **Buddhism and Jainism**: These religious movements rejected the Varna system, promoting equality and non-discrimination, with leaders like Buddha and Mahavira coming from non-Brahminical, lower-caste backgrounds.

- **Non-Vedic Populations**: The *Nishadas* and other forest-dwelling or non-Aryan groups were not incorporated into the Varna system and followed their own traditions, often beyond Brahminical influence.

- **Kshatriya Kings from Non-Brahminical Backgrounds**: Rulers like Chandragupta Maurya and the Magadha kings were from non-Brahminical, non-Kshatriya backgrounds, showing that not all rulers adhered to the Varna system.

- **Urban Populations**: In urban centers like Pataliputra and Taxila, the influence of Brahminical Varna norms was weaker, and trade, commerce, and various occupations were more fluid

Ans - 6.)

- **Succession to Power**: In royal and elite families, succession was typically through the male line, ensuring that power and wealth passed from father to son, as seen in the dynastic succession of kingdoms like the Magadha and Maurya empires.

- **Marriage Alliances**: Elite families used marriage as a strategy to maintain or enhance their social status, with daughters often married off to strengthen political ties, while property and lineage were passed through the male heirs.

- **Brahminical Influence**: The rise of Brahminical orthodoxy also reinforced patriliny, with rituals and sacrifices often requiring male descendants to maintain ancestral traditions and privileges.

- **Status and Property Inheritance**: Land and property were typically inherited through male heirs, strengthening the role of the patrilineal family in securing economic and social position in society.

- **Example - Kshatriya Rulers**: Kshatriya rulers, like those of the Magadha kingdom (Bimbisara and Ajatashatru), ensured the continuation of their rule through their male descendants

Ans- 7.)

- **Social Structure**: The *Mahabharata* reflects the complex social structure of ancient India, with its emphasis on family roles, inheritance, and succession.

- **Conflict over Succession**: The epic highlights the struggle over inheritance and power within royal families, such as the conflict between the Kauravas and Pandavas.

- **Marriage Alliances**: It provides insights into how marriages were used for political alliances and consolidating power, as seen in Draupadi's marriage to the Pandavas.

- **Patriarchal Norms**: The epic illustrates patriarchal practices, where the family head had control over inheritance, leadership, and decision-making.

- **Role of Women**: The *Mahabharata* explores the roles and status of women in familial and political contexts, with characters like Kunti and Draupadi playing pivotal roles.

- **Kinship and Duty**: The text emphasizes kinship obligations, where familial duty often conflicted with personal desires and moral choices, shaping key events in the narrative

Ans - 8.)

- **Excavation at Hastinapura**: B.B. Lal, an archaeologist, conducted excavations at Hastinapura (modern-day in Uttar Pradesh) during the 1950s and 1960s.

- **Evidence of Ancient Settlement**: His excavations revealed evidence of an ancient settlement that aligned with the descriptions of Hastinapura in the *Mahabharata*.

- **Layered Findings**: Lal uncovered multiple layers of habitation, including pottery, tools, and remnants of structures, indicating continuous occupation over centuries.

- **Archaeological Significance**: These findings suggested that Hastinapura was not just a mythical city, but a real, historically significant urban center.

- **Dating the Site**: The pottery and other artifacts found at the site were dated to approximately the 2nd millennium BCE, supporting the possibility of the *Mahabharata*'s events taking place during this period.

- **Link to the Mahabharata**: While the discoveries could not definitively confirm the *Mahabharata* events, they provided archaeological evidence of settlements that could have been the basis for the epic's narrative

Ans – 9.)

1. **Main Narrative (Bharata)**: This is the core story of the *Mahabharata*, focusing on the conflict between the Pandavas and Kauravas.

2. **Didactic Sections (Smriti)**: These include sections that offer moral and philosophical teachings, such as the *Bhagavad Gita*.

- The original story was probably composed by charioteer-bards known as sutas who generally accompanied Kshatriya warriors to the battlefield and composed poems celebrating their victories and other achievements.

- **Author**: The *Mahabharata* is traditionally attributed to the sage **Vyasa**.
- **Original Language**: The text was originally composed in **Sanskrit**

Ans - 10.)

- **Patrilineal System**: Property and land were mostly inherited through the male line, favoring men in terms of ownership and control.

- **Women's Limited Rights**: Women generally had limited access to land and property, with inheritance usually passing to sons or male heirs.

- **Brahminical Influence**: The rise of Brahminical norms reinforced patriarchal structures, restricting women's rights to property.

- **Marital Property**: In some cases, women could have access to property through dowries, but this was often controlled by their husbands or male family members.

- **Buddhist and Jain Influence**: Both Buddhist and Jain texts suggest more egalitarian views towards women, though practical limitations on property rights still existed.

- **Queen's Role**: In royal families, queens sometimes had control over land, but this was often due to their status as consorts and not as a norm for all women.

- **Legal Texts**: Some legal texts allowed women to own property, but this was usually linked to specific circumstances, like widowhood or being a daughter without brothers.

- **Rural Context**: In rural societies, women's role in agriculture was vital, but their control over land was limited by patriarchal practices

Ans - 11.)

- **Dynasty**: Gotami Puta Siri Satakani was a prominent ruler of the **Satavahana dynasty**.

- **Reign**: He ruled around the 1st century BCE, expanding the Satavahana influence in the Deccan

- **Title**: The title *Gotami Puta* signifies that he was the son of Gotami, indicating the maternal line's importance.

- **Territorial Control**: His empire covered large parts of present-day Andhra Pradesh, Maharashtra, and Karnataka.

- **Administration**: He maintained a decentralized administrative system, with local rulers enjoying some autonomy under the central authority.

- **Coins**: Satakani issued coins, which helped in understanding his political and economic history.

- **Cultural Patronage**: He supported both Brahmanical and Buddhist traditions, highlighting religious tolerance

Ans-12.)

1. **Varna**:
     - Refers to the four broad, hierarchical categories of society: **Brahmins** (priests), **Kshatriyas** (warriors), **Vaishyas** (merchants), and **Shudras** (laborers).
     - It is a theoretical, idealized classification often described in ancient texts like the *Rigveda* and *Manusmriti*.

2. **Jati**:
     - Refers to the numerous sub-castes or smaller groups within the Varna system, based on specific occupations, region, and social practices.
     - Jatis were more fluid and practical in nature, and the boundaries between them were often more flexible compared to the rigid Varna system.
     -

Varna is a broad and theoretical classification, while **Jati** represents the actual social divisions

Note – The Remaining questions are for your practice, hence their solutions aren't provided, Keep Practicing..!

Chapter – 4 (Thinkers, Beliefs and Buildings)

Ans – 1.)

Buddha, also known as **Siddhartha Gautama**, was the founder of **Buddhism**, one of the major world religions. He is regarded as an enlightened teacher who spread the principles of peace, wisdom, and non-violence

Early Life:

- Siddhartha Gautama was born in **Lumbini** (present-day Nepal) around the 6th century BCE, in a royal family of the **Shakya clan**.

- He was shielded from the harsh realities of life by his father, King Suddhodana, who wanted to protect him from any suffering.

- After encountering sickness, old age, death, and ascetics during his visits outside the palace, Siddhartha was deeply moved and decided to leave his royal life in search of the truth.

- He renounced his kingdom, family, and luxurious life at the age of 29 to seek enlightenment

Major Teachings: Four Noble Truths

  - Life involves suffering (**dukkha**).
  - Suffering is caused by desire and attachment
  - There is a way to end suffering.
  - The way to end suffering is through the **Eightfold Path**

- **The Eightfold Path**: This is a guide to ethical and mental development, consisting of right understanding, intention, speech, action, livelihood, effort, mindfulness, and concentration.

- **Doctrine of Middle Way**: Buddha advocated for a balanced life, avoiding both extreme self-indulgence and extreme asceticism.

- **Nirvana**: The ultimate goal of Buddhism, representing the cessation of suffering and the attainment of enlightenment, where one is free from the cycle of rebirth (samsara).

- **Non-Violence and Compassion**: Buddha emphasized **ahimsa** (non-violence) and the practice of compassion towards all living beings

Ans-2.)

- **Reaction to Vedic Tradition**: Both religions emerged as alternatives to the rigid rituals and caste system of the Vedic religion, appealing to those dissatisfied with Brahmanical practices.

- **Message of Equality**: Both Buddhism and Jainism promoted **equality** and rejected the caste system, making them accessible to a wider audience, including the lower classes.

- **Simple and Practical Teachings**: They offered simple, practical paths to spiritual enlightenment, focusing on personal experience rather than ritualistic worship.

- **Support from Rulers**: The patronage of influential rulers, such as Emperor **Ashoka** for Buddhism and King **Chandraprapta Maurya** for Jainism, helped in their widespread adoption.

- **Social and Economic Changes**: Urbanization, trade, and the rise of new towns created a need for new religious ideas, making these non-Vedic traditions more appealing.

- **Appeal to Common People**: Both religions rejected elaborate rituals and emphasized **individual effort** for spiritual growth, attracting followers from diverse social backgrounds.

- **Spread of Monastic Communities**: Both religions established monastic orders, which helped in the spread of their ideas through organized missionary work.

- **Rejection of Rituals**: Both rejected elaborate Vedic rituals and sacrifices, offering a more accessible and personal form of spirituality

Ans-3.)

Main Features of the Stupa at Sanchi-

- **Structure**: The **Stupa at Sanchi** is a large hemispherical dome built to house relics of the Buddha. It is one of the oldest and best-preserved examples of ancient Indian architecture.

- **Toranas (Gateways)**: The stupa is surrounded by **four elaborately carved gateways** (toranas), which depict scenes from the life of Buddha and Jataka tales (stories of Buddha's previous lives). These are important for understanding Buddhist art and symbolism.

- **Reliefs and Sculptures**: The stupa features intricate **reliefs and sculptures** on the gateways, depicting Buddha in symbolic forms like footprints, the Bodhi tree, or the wheel of Dharma.

- **Symbolism**: The stupa represents the Buddha's teachings, with the **dome** symbolizing the universe and the **pillar** representing the axis of the world.

- **Shrine**: The stupa houses relics of Buddha, typically inside a small chamber,

Role of Rulers of Bhopal in Preserving the Stupa –

- **Restoration Efforts**: The **rulers of Bhopal**, particularly during the 19th century, played a significant role in preserving and restoring the Sanchi Stupa, which had fallen into disrepair over the centuries.

- **Efforts by Sir John Marshall**: Under the patronage of the Bhopal rulers, **Sir John Marshall** and the Archaeological Survey of India, significant restoration work was done at the site.

- **Promotion of Cultural Heritage**: The rulers supported the identification and promotion of Sanchi as a key cultural and religious monument, which contributed to its global recognition and preservation

Ans – 4.) Philosophy: Jainism emphasizes the principles of **non-violence (ahimsa), truth (satya)**, and **asceticism**. It believes that the soul is eternal and can attain liberation (moksha) by eliminating all karmic attachments.

Major Teachings in Jainism:

- **Ahimsa (Non-Violence)**: Jainism stresses absolute non-violence in thoughts, words, and actions. It extends beyond human beings to include all living creatures.

- **Satya (Truth)**: Practicing truthfulness in every aspect of life and speech.

- **Non-Possessiveness**: Advocating detachment from material possessions and desires, focusing instead on spiritual growth.

- **Non-Absolutism**: The belief that truth is multifaceted, and different perspectives should be respected. This teaching promotes tolerance and understanding.

- **Asceticism**: Emphasis on self-discipline, renunciation of worldly pleasures, and meditation as a means to purify the soul.

- **Karma and Rebirth**: Jainism teaches that every action results in karma, which binds the soul to the cycle of birth, death, and rebirth. Liberation is achieved by purging oneself of karma through ethical living and spiritual practices.

- **Path to Liberation**: The ultimate goal of Jainism is to achieve liberation (moksha) from the cycle of birth and rebirth by following strict ethical conduct, meditation, and asceticism.

- **Tirthankaras**: Jainism believes in 24 **Tirthankaras** who are revered spiritual teachers- **Mahavira**

Ans - 5.)

- **Period of Growth**: Puranic Hinduism grew during the early medieval period (4th-7th centuries CE).

- **Influence of the Puranas**: The **Puranas** (ancient texts) popularized the worship of deities like **Vishnu**, **Shiva**, and **Devi**, and spread myths and rituals.

- **Sectarian Worship**: Promoted the worship of specific deities, leading to the rise of sects devoted to **Vishnu**, **Shiva**, and **Shakti**.

- **Philosophical Development**: Philosophical schools like **Vedanta**, **Yoga**, and **Sankhya** contributed to the growth of Hindu thought, with **Bhakti** (devotion) gaining prominence.

- **Role of Temples**: Temples became central to religious life, serving as hubs for **worship**, **pilgrimages**, and **rituals**.

- **Cultural Impact**: Temples fostered art, architecture, and community life, becoming significant in shaping social and cultural practices.

- **Inclusive Worship**: Temples made religious practices more accessible to a broader section of society beyond the priestly class.

- **Kingly Patronage**: Kings supported the building of temples, making them focal points of cultural and political life.

Ans - 6.)

- **Historical Significance**: The **Sanchi Stupa**, built by **Emperor Ashoka**, is one of the oldest and most important Buddhist structures in India.

- **Architectural Excellence**: It is renowned for its **architecture**, including the **toranas** (gateways), which are intricately carved with scenes from the **life of Buddha**.

- **Preservation**: The stupa was largely preserved due to **limited human intervention** and continuous care, particularly during the reign of the **Mughal and British periods**.

- **Cultural Heritage**: It remains a key symbol of **Buddhist art** and **architecture**, showcasing the **rich history** of early Indian Buddhism.

- **UNESCO World Heritage Site**: Sanchi was declared a **UNESCO World Heritage Site** in 1989 due to its **historical, religious, and cultural importance**.

- **Role of Local Rulers**: The **rulers of Bhopal** played a significant role in its preservation, taking efforts to protect and maintain the stupa in modern times.

- **Continued Pilgrimage Site**: The stupa continues to be an important site for **Buddhist pilgrims**, further ensuring its preservation

Ans – 7.)

- **Rise of New Religions**: This period witnessed the emergence of **Buddhism** and **Jainism**, which introduced new philosophies and ways of thinking about life, suffering, and salvation.

- **Philosophical Developments**: **Greek philosophy** blossomed with thinkers like **Socrates, Plato**, and **Aristotle**, contributing to the development of **rational thought** and **logic** in the West.

- **Political Changes**: The formation of large empires, such as the **Mauryan Empire** in India and the **Persian Empire**, signified a shift toward centralized political systems and governance.

- **Cultural Exchanges**: Increased trade and interactions across the **Silk Route** and **Mediterranean**, fostering cross-cultural exchanges and spreading ideas, art, and religion.

- **Social Reforms**: The period saw challenges to traditional social structures, with the rise of **non-Brahmanical** and **non-aristocratic** movements, leading to changes in social hierarchies.

- **Scientific Advancements**: Major advancements in **astronomy**, **mathematics**, and **medicine** occurred, influencing the future development of scientific thought.

- **Urbanization and Trade**: Growing urban centers and long-distance trade routes transformed economies and connected distant cultures

Ans – 8.) Answer would be same as above mentioned Answer - 1 (Thinkers, Beliefs and Buildings)

Ans – 9.) • **Concept of Savior**: In Hinduism, the notion of a savior is often embodied in the form of **Avatars** of gods, especially **Vishnu**, who descends to earth to restore cosmic order.

- **Vishnu's Avatars**: Vishnu's **Ten Avatars (Dashavatara)**, including **Rama** and **Krishna**, are considered divine incarnations sent to save humanity from chaos, evil, and injustice.

- **Role of the Savior**: The savior figures in Hinduism restore **Dharma** (righteousness) and protect the world from **Adharma** (unrighteousness), guiding people towards moral and spiritual growth.

- **Bhakti Movement Influence**: The Bhakti movement emphasized the personal devotion to the savior deities, especially **Krishna** and **Rama**, as a means to attain salvation and divine protection.

- **Mythological Tales**: Stories of divine interventions by gods or heroes, like in the **Mahabharata** and **Ramayana**, highlight the savior's role in overcoming adversity and protecting the dharma

Ans – 10.)

- **Vedic Sacrifices**: In ancient India, the sacrificial tradition began with **Vedic rituals**, primarily involving offerings to gods, performed by priests (Brahmins) for the welfare of society.

- **Types of Sacrifices**: Key sacrifices included the **Yajna**, such as **Agnihotra** and **Ashvamedha** (horse sacrifice), which were meant to ensure cosmic order and prosperity.

- **Brahmanical Evolution**: Over time, sacrifices evolved into more elaborate rituals detailed in the **Brahmanas** and **Upanishads**, with an emphasis on the **spiritual and philosophical significance** of the rites.

- **Rise of Philosophical Reflection**: By the later Vedic period, sacrifices began to be seen not only as external rituals but as symbolic acts for **spiritual purification** and **knowledge**.

- **Decline in Jainism and Buddhism**: With the rise of **Jainism** and **Buddhism**, the sacrificial practices were challenged, as both religions rejected animal sacrifices and emphasized non-violence.

- **Puranic Sacrifices**: In the **Puranic** period, the sacrificial tradition persisted but became more focused on **devotional worship** (Bhakti) rather than grand rituals, highlighting personal devotion over formal sacrifices.

- **Evolving into Ritualistic Worship**: Over time, these sacrifices evolved into **ritualistic temple worship** and **festivals**, with the focus shifting towards the **offering of food, fruits**, and **flowers** rather than elaborate sacrifices

Ans – 11.) • **Rejection of Vedic Rituals**: Both **Buddhism** and **Jainism** rejected the complex Vedic rituals and sacrifices that were central to the **Brahminical system**, offering simpler paths to spiritual liberation.

- **Emphasis on Individual Effort**: These religions emphasized **personal effort** and **self-discipline** over reliance on priests and rituals, making them accessible to a wider population.

- **Non-Violence (Ahimsa): Jainism**, in particular, promoted **Ahimsa** (non-violence)

- **Social Equality**: Both **Buddhism** and **Jainism** provided a more **egalitarian** approach, welcoming followers from various social strata, including lower castes, unlike the rigid caste hierarchy in the Brahminical system.

- **Appeal to Urban Populations**: These religions appealed to urban dwellers and merchant communities, offering practical solutions for moral and ethical living, which complemented their economic and social aspirations.

- **Charismatic Leaders**: Figures like **Buddha** and **Mahavira** were charismatic leaders who promoted a **simple, direct path to enlightenment**, which attracted many followers.

- **Monastic Communities**: Both religions established **monastic communities** (Sanghas), where people could pursue spiritual learning, meditation, and a disciplined lifestyle, making it an organized, alternative system to Brahminical authority.

- **Spread of Ideas**: The **support of kings** like **Ashoka** for Buddhism, and the patronage by merchant classes for both religions, helped in spreading their teachings widely across the subcontinent

Ans – 12.)

- **Monastic Community (Sangha)**: Buddha's followers formed a **Sangha**, a community of monks and nuns, dedicated to the practice and teaching of **Buddha's teachings** (Dhamma).

- **Lay Followers**: In addition to the monastic community, there were **lay followers** who supported the Sangha and practiced Buddhism in daily life, striving for moral conduct and spiritual growth.

- **Diverse Support**: Buddha's followers came from various social backgrounds, including **merchants**, **farmers**, and even **royalty**, making Buddhism a religion accessible to all.

- **Women in the Sangha**: Buddha allowed **women** to join the Sangha, creating a separate order for nuns (Bhikkhunis), which was progressive for the time.

- **Kings and Rulers**: Several rulers, like **Emperor Ashoka**, embraced Buddhism and promoted its teachings, helping to spread it across the Indian subcontinent and beyond.

- **Missionaries**: Buddha's followers, particularly **disciples** like **Ananda**, spread his teachings through **missionary work** across different regions, ensuring the religion's growth.

- **Devotional Followers**: Along with those who followed the monastic path, many devotees also followed **Buddha's teachings** through **prayers**, **rituals**, and **pilgrimages** to holy sites like **Bodh Gaya**

Ans – 13.)

- **Relics of Buddha**: Stupas were built to **house relics** (physical remains) of **Buddha** or other significant Buddhist figures, as a mark of respect and reverence.

- **Symbol of Buddha's Enlightenment**: Stupas symbolized **Buddha's enlightenment** and his teachings, serving as a focal point for meditation and worship.

- **Pilgrimage Sites**: Stupas became important **pilgrimage destinations** for Buddhists, where they could pay homage to the relics and the Buddha's life.

- **Spiritual Merit**: Circumambulating stupas was believed to earn **spiritual merit** and help in the pursuit of **Nirvana** (liberation from the cycle of rebirth).

- **Preservation of Teachings**: Stupas helped in the **preservation** and **dissemination of Buddhist teachings**, with inscriptions and carvings depicting important events from Buddha's life.

- **Cultural Integration**: Stupas served as a means of **spreading Buddhism** across regions, with each stupa being a focal point for the Buddhist community and its teachings.

- **Architectural Significance**: Stupas, like the **Sanchi Stupa**, are important examples of ancient **Buddhist architecture**, reflecting the culture and artistic developments of the time.

- **Symbol of Unity**: Stupas represented the **unity of the Buddhist community** and their shared commitment to the principles of Buddhism

Ans – 14.)

- **Dome (Anda)**: The main part of the stupa, representing the **cosmos** or **Buddha's mind**. It is a hemispherical dome that houses the relics.

- **Foundation**: The base of the stupa, symbolizing the **firm foundation** of the Buddha's teachings.

- **Chattra (Umbrella)**: on top, representing the **Buddha's protection** and **spiritual power**.

- **Mast** - yashti surrounded by unbrella

- **Harmika**: A small platform at the top of the stupa, often enclosed by a railing, symbolizing the **abode of gods** or the **ultimate reality**.

- **Toranas (Gateways)**: Elaborate carved **gateways** at the cardinal points of the stupa, often depicting scenes from **Buddha's life** and important **Buddhist motifs**

Chapter – 5 (Thinkers, Beliefs and Buildings)

Ans – 1.)

- **Road Networks**: Ibn Battuta described the extensive **road networks** in the **14th century**, which were crucial for trade and communication.

- **Postal System**: He observed the presence of a well-organized **postal system** that helped in maintaining communication across vast regions.

- **Caravanserais**: Ibn Battuta highlighted the role of **caravanserais** (resting places for travelers) that facilitated long-distance travel and ensured the safety of merchants and travelers.

- **Official Communication**: He noted that **letters** and **documents** were often carried by **messengers** or **couriers** who ensured the efficient transmission of information.

- **Trade and Cultural Exchange**: The **communication system** played a vital role in fostering **trade** and **cultural exchanges** between different regions in the **Islamic world**

Ans – 2.)

- Ibn Battuta praised **Delhi** as a prosperous and vibrant city with a bustling **marketplace**

- He highlighted its **grand architecture**, particularly the **Sultanate buildings**, and noted the city's importance as a **political and cultural hub**.

- Battuta described **Delhi's ruler, Muhammad bin Tughlaq**, as being both **ambitious** and **innovative** but also criticized his **harsh rule** at times.

- Ibn Battuta remarked on **Daulatabad** (under Muhammad bin Tughlaq's rule) as a **fortified city** with a **strategic location**, chosen by the Sultan to relocate the capital from Delhi.

- He found the **city's layout** and the **harsh decision** of shifting the capital there to be **difficult** and **inconvenient** for the people, noting the long and challenging journey.

- He was critical of the **logistical challenges** and the **disruption caused** by the capital shift to Daulatabad, viewing it as a **failed experiment**.

Ans – 3.)

- **Bernier** emphasized that in **Mughal India**, the **land was considered the property of the emperor** (the **crown**), and the **ruler controlled all land revenues**.

- He noted that land was not privately owned by individuals but was **leased to cultivators** or **landlords** who paid taxes to the crown

- **Bernier** observed that **private ownership of land** did not exist in the same way as it did in **Europe**. People did not hold land as their personal property; rather, they had **temporary rights to use the land** under the emperor's authority.

- He pointed out that **individuals** could not sell or freely transfer land as private property; instead, it was tied to the **state's control**, and ownership was a **subject to royal policy** and **revenue assessments**

Ans – 4.)

- **Comprehensive Description of India**:

  - *Kitab-ul-Hind* is a detailed account of Indian **culture, religion, society, geography**, and **science**, written by **Al-Biruni** in the 11th century.

- **Objective and Analytical Approach**:

  - Al-Biruni adopted an **objective and analytical approach**, contrasting Indian practices with those of the **Persian world** and other cultures, aiming to understand rather than criticize.

- **Focus on Religion and Philosophy**:

  - The text explores **Hinduism**, its **rituals**, **philosophical ideas**, and **belief systems**, offering insights into Indian religious practices and beliefs, including a study of various **Hindu texts**.

- **Cultural Comparisons**:

  - Al-Biruni compared **Indian traditions** with those of the **Greeks**, **Persians**, and other cultures, highlighting the distinctiveness of Indian ways of life.

- **Use of Source Material**:

  - Al-Biruni used **direct observations**, **Indian texts**, and **discussions with scholars** to compile the information, making the work a valuable source of historical knowledge.

- **Scientific Contributions**: The work also touches upon **Indian astronomy**, **mathematics**, and **medicine**, reflecting Al-Biruni's interest in Indian scientific achievements.

- **Cultural Sensitivity**:

  - Al-Biruni approached the study of India with respect for its culture, understanding its complexities, and avoiding harsh criticism, which distinguished his work from many others of his time

Ans – 5.)

- **Arrival in Delhi**:

  - Ibn Battuta arrived in **Delhi** in **1333 CE** and was impressed by the **grandeur of the city** and its **prosperity** under the rule of **Muhammad bin Tughlaq**.

- **Impressions of Delhi**:

  - He described **Delhi** as a **cosmopolitan city**, with people from different regions and backgrounds. The **marketplaces** were bustling, and the **royal court** was noted for its grandeur and wealth.

- **Royal Court of Muhammad bin Tughlaq**:

  - Ibn Battuta admired the **king's hospitality** but criticized his **administrative decisions**, particularly the **transfer of capital to Daulatabad**, which he thought was impractical.

- **Journey to Daulatabad**:

  - Ibn Battuta followed the king's order to shift to **Daulatabad**, a move he considered **harsh** and **burdensome** for the people due to its **geographical challenges**.

- **Religious Tolerance**:

  - He observed the **religious tolerance** of the Delhi Sultanate, as Muslims, Hindus, and others coexisted, although he did mention the **persecution of certain groups**.

- **Administration and Justice**:

  - Ibn Battuta appreciated the **strict justice system**, especially the **functioning of the Qazi (Islamic judge)**, and the **efficiency** of the administrative structure in the empire.

- **Cultural Observations** - He noted the **customs** and **traditions** of the people, including their dress, food, and social behaviors, providing a glimpse into **medieval Indian society**.

- **Challenges and Difficulties**:

  - His travels faced **difficulties** like **poor roads**, **harsh climates**, and the **long distance** between cities, yet he found these challenges an integral part of his adventure.

- **Return to Morocco**:

  - After many years in India, Ibn Battuta eventually returned to **Morocco** in **1349 CE**, having witnessed the vast expanse and diversity of the **Indian subcontinent**

Ans – 6.)

- **Time Period**:

  - Ibn Battuta visited India in the **14th century (1330s)**, while **Francois Bernier** arrived in **17th century (1650s)**.

- **Cultural Approach**:

  - Ibn Battuta was more **admiring** of Indian culture and found it **fascinating**, while Bernier had a more **critical and judgmental** view, especially of the Mughal system.

- **Religious Views**:

  - Ibn Battuta was a **devout Muslim**, often focusing on religious practices and customs, while Bernier, a **French physician**, was more **observant** of **political and economic** aspects.

- **Experience of Mughal Court**:

  - Ibn Battuta admired the **luxury** and **administrative system** of the Sultanate and Mughals, whereas Bernier **criticized the Mughal court's extravagance** and **inefficiency**.

- **Perspective on Land Ownership**:

  - Bernier was critical of the **Mughal system of crown ownership of land** and the **lack of private property**, which he saw as a barrier to economic progress. Ibn Battuta did not emphasize this issue as much.

- **Social Hierarchy**: Ibn Battuta noted the **social diversity** in India, including interactions among Muslims, Hindus, and other groups, while Bernier focused more on the **rigid caste system** and **inequalities** in society.

- **Travel Experience**:

  - Ibn Battuta enjoyed the **adventure of traveling**, whereas Bernier seemed more concerned with **political and social stability** during his travels in India.

Ans – 7.)

- **Complexity of the Caste System**:

  - Al-Biruni observed that the **caste system** in India was **complex** and strictly adhered to, with little scope for **social mobility**.

- **Social Stratification**:

  - He noted that people were **born into specific castes** (varnas), and their **occupations and social status** were determined by their caste.

- **Rigid Social Boundaries**:

  - Al-Biruni remarked on the **rigid boundaries** between the castes, where individuals of different castes rarely interacted socially or shared the same spaces.

- **Lack of Social Equality**:

  - He criticized the **inequality** inherent in the caste system, highlighting the **lower status** of certain groups, especially the **Shudras** and **untouchables**.

- **Religious Justification**:

  - Al-Biruni acknowledged that the caste system was **justified by religious texts** and that it had deep **religious significance** in the Indian society.

- **Cultural Isolation**:

  - He observed that the caste system created a form of **cultural isolation**, limiting **interactions** and **intermarriage** between different castes

Ans - 8.)

- **Status of Women**:

  - Women in medieval India were often (not always) **confined to domestic roles** and had limited **freedom**. Their rights were largely **restricted** by social norms and the caste system.

- **Sati (Self-Immolation)**:

  - **Sati** was a **widow's practice** where a woman would **immolate herself** on her husband's funeral pyre. Travelers like **Ibn Battuta** and **Bernier** noted the **existence** of this practice, though it was not universally practiced.

- **Social Constraints**:

  - Women faced **social restrictions**, including the practice of **purdah** (seclusion) and the **restriction of mobility**, which was especially prevalent in the **upper classes**.

- **Marriage**:

  - **Early marriages** were common, and women were often **married off at a young age**, while **dowries** were expected in many cases.

- **Role of Slaves**:

  - Slavery was prevalent, and **slaves** were often **captured in wars** or were **indentured** for economic reasons. Slaves were forced to perform **manual labor** and serve their masters, with little to no personal rights.

- **Exploitation of Slaves**:

  - Slaves were subjected to **harsh conditions** and had no social or legal protections. Their **freedom** was severely limited, and they were considered **property** rather than people

Ans – 9.)

- **Crown Ownership of Land**:

  - Bernier noted that **land was considered the property of the king** in Mughal India, with **no private land ownership**. This meant the **government** had ultimate control over land distribution and taxes.

- **Social Stratification**:

  - He observed that **Indian society was deeply hierarchical** and **divided into castes**, with **rigid social divisions** that affected every aspect of life.

- **Economic Disparities**:

  - Bernier emphasized the **vast economic inequalities** in India, with a **small elite** living in luxury while the majority of the population lived in **poverty** and **squalor**.

- **Corruption in Administration**:

  - He criticized the **corruption** and **inefficiency** in the **Mughal administration**, particularly the **abuses of power** by officials and the **mismanagement** of the empire's resources.

- **Luxury of the Elite**:

  - Bernier highlighted the **extravagant lifestyles** of the Mughal elite and the **luxuries of the court**, contrasting sharply with the conditions of the common people.

- **Religious Toleration**:

  - He acknowledged the **religious tolerance** in the Mughal Empire, noting that different communities, including **Hindus, Muslims, and others**, coexisted relatively peacefully, though there were tensions at times

- **Lack of Private Land Ownership**:

  - Bernier argued that the **absence of private property** in land prevented the rise of **landlords who could improve and cultivate the land**, leading to economic stagnation.

- **Negative View of Mughal Empire**:

  - He described the Mughal Empire as a realm of **"beggars and barbarians"**, where **cities were ruined**, towns were plagued by **bad air**, and **fields were overgrown with bushes and marshes**.

- **"Camp Towns"**:

  - Despite his criticisms, Bernier described Mughal cities as **"camp towns"**, which existed primarily to serve the needs of the **imperial camp**, highlighting their dependence on the **royal court** for survival

Ans – 10.)

Al-Biruni

- **Background**:

  - Al-Biruni was a **Persian scholar**, scientist, and traveler who visited **India** in the early 11th century during the reign of **Mahmud of Ghazni**.

- **Main Work**:

  - His most famous work is **"Kitab-ul-Hind"** (Book of India), where he extensively described **Indian culture, geography, religion**, and society based on his observations.

- **Views on Indian Society**:

  - Al-Biruni showed **great respect** for Indian knowledge, particularly its **mathematics** and **astronomy**. He critically analyzed the **caste system** and **Hindu religious practices**, presenting them with a sense of objectivity.

- **Perspective on Caste System**:

  - He was keen to understand **India's caste system** and **varna system**, which he found to be complex but integral to social organization

Ibn Battuta

- **Background**:

  - Ibn Battuta was a **Moroccan traveler** and scholar who journeyed across much of the **Islamic world** and **India** in the 14th century.

- **Views on India**:

  - He praised the **prosperity** of **Delhi** but was critical of the **Mongol raids** and other social issues like the **practice of Sati** and **the status of women**.

- **Delhi and Daulatabad**:

  - Ibn Battuta had contrasting views of **Delhi** and **Daulatabad**. While he found Delhi to be **impressive**, he described Daulatabad as a **difficult and desolate place** due to its strategic relocation.

- **Mughal Administration**:

- He admired the **sultanate system** in India, especially the **strong control of Muhammad bin Tughlaq**

Francois Bernier

- **Background**:

  - **Francois Bernier** was a **French physician** and traveler who visited **India** in the 17th century and later wrote about his observations in **"Travels in the Mughal Empire"**.

- **Criticism of Mughal Empire**:

  - He was **critical** of the **Mughal administration**, especially the **land ownership system**. He believed the **lack of private property** in land led to **economic stagnation** and no progress in agriculture.

- **Mughal Society**:

  - Bernier viewed the Mughal Empire as a realm of **"beggars" and "barbarians"**, where **cities** were **ruined** and **fields** were underutilized.

- **Perspective on Land and Wealth**:

  - He claimed that the **crown ownership** of land prevented the emergence of a class of **"improving landlords"**, which he considered detrimental to the empire's prosperity

Note – The Remaining questions are for your practice, hence their solutions aren't provided, Keep Practicing..!

Chapter – 6 (Bhakti and Sufi Traditions)

Ans – 1.) The **Lingayat tradition** emerged in the 12th century in Karnataka, primarily under the leadership of **Basava**, a social reformer and religious leader. It is a distinctive form of **Bhakti movement** that rejected traditional caste-based rituals and practices, emphasizing direct devotion to **Shiva** in the form of **Ishtalinga**.

Key teachings and philosophy of **Lingayat tradition** –

- **Emphasis on Bhakti**:

    - Devotion to **Lord Shiva** is central, with followers believing in the **direct worship** of Shiva through the **linga** (a small, portable stone symbol of Shiva).

- **Rejection of Caste System**:

    - The Lingayats rejected the rigid **varna (caste) system**, promoting the idea that all people, regardless of caste, could attain spiritual liberation through devotion to Shiva.

- **Non-Brahminical Practices**:

    - They opposed the Brahmanical rituals and priesthood, focusing instead on personal devotion, ethics, and moral living.

- **Equality of All**:

    - The philosophy of **equality** and **social justice** was central to their teachings, challenging the prevailing social hierarchies of the time.

- **Philosophical Teachings**:

    - The tradition emphasized **self-realization** and the **importance of inner purity**. **Basava's** vachanas (poetic hymns) expressed these ideas, encouraging a life of simplicity, humility, and devotion.

- **Rejection of Rituals**:

    - Lingayats rejected the necessity of temple worship, sacred threads, and other orthodox rituals. The primary focus was on internal devotion and the **meditation on the linga**.

- **Ideal of Social Reform**:

    - Basava and his followers advocated for social reform, particularly in areas of **gender equality**, **social justice**, and **economic equality**, promoting a more inclusive and egalitarian society

Ans – 2.)

- **Early Life**:

  - **Mirabai** (1498–1547) was a Rajput princess from Merta (Rajasthan), born into a royal family but rejected the traditional aristocratic lifestyle for devotion to **Lord Krishna**.

- **Devotion to Krishna**:

  - She is known for her **unwavering devotion to Krishna**, often expressing her love through **bhajans** (devotional songs) and **poems** dedicated to him.

- **Rejection of Social Norms**:

  - Mirabai defied societal expectations, including rejecting the role of a traditional wife, and faced immense opposition for her commitment to Krishna over her marital duties.

- **Role in Bhakti Movement**:

  - She played a key role in the **Bhakti movement**, promoting **personal devotion (bhakti)** over ritualistic practices, and highlighting the importance of direct connection with the divine.

- **Spiritual Poems and Bhajans**:

  - She composed numerous **bhajans** and **poems** in **Hindi** and **Rajasthani**, which expressed her love for Krishna, and challenged societal norms, especially regarding women.

- **Inspiration to Women**:

  - Mirabai became a symbol of **female empowerment** and **spiritual freedom**, inspiring women to transcend traditional roles and express their spiritual devotion independently.

- **Legacy**:

  - Her work and life left a lasting impact on the **Bhakti movement**, and she is remembered as one of the **prominent female saints** and poets in medieval India.

- **Connection with Folk Tradition**:

  - Mirabai's **bhajans** were widely sung and became part of the popular **folk tradition**, transcending regional and cultural boundaries

Ans – 3.)

- **Emphasis on a Personal Connection with God**:

  - Kabir emphasized the importance of **direct devotion** to **God** (Ram, Allah, or the formless one) over rituals and idol worship, advocating for a personal, inner connection with the divine.

- **Criticism of Rituals**:

  - He was a vocal critic of both **Hindu** and **Muslim** rituals, particularly idol worship and the caste system, arguing that **faith and devotion** were more important than external practices.

- **Unity of God**:

  - Kabir believed in the **oneness of God**, rejecting the division between Hinduism and Islam, often using both **Hindu** and **Muslim** terminology in his teachings, reflecting his inclusive and syncretic view of religion.

- **Rejection of Caste System**:

  - He strongly opposed the **caste system** and social discrimination, teaching that all people, regardless of their caste, are equal in the eyes of God.

- **Importance of a Guru**:

  - Kabir stressed the role of the **Guru** (spiritual teacher) as the guide to spiritual enlightenment, teaching that true wisdom and knowledge come from a realized teacher rather than ritualistic learning.

- **Poetry and Hymns**:

  - Kabir's teachings are found in his **dohe** (couplets) and **bhajans**, which are simple yet profound, and they focus on themes like **devotion**, **inner purity**, and **self-realization**.

- **God is formless**:

  - He believed in a **formless God**, often referring to the divine as **Nirguna** (without attributes), rejecting the idea of God in any physical form.

- **Emphasis on Love and Compassion**:

  - Kabir's philosophy encouraged living a life of **love, compassion**, and **humility**, and he emphasized the importance of **selfless service** to humanity.

Ans -4.) • **Oneness of God**:

- Guru Nanak emphasized the belief in a **single, formless, and eternal God** (Ik Onkar), who is beyond human understanding but present in all creation.

- **Equality of All People**:

  - He promoted the idea of **equality** and **brotherhood** among all people, rejecting caste distinctions, social hierarchies, and gender discrimination.

- **Rejection of Rituals**:

  - Guru Nanak rejected empty rituals and superstitions, advocating for **true devotion** to God through **good deeds, honest living**, and **selfless service**.

- **Importance of Naam Simran**:

  - He emphasized the practice of **Naam Simran** (meditation on God's name), as a way to achieve spiritual purity and connect with the divine.

- **Social Justice**:

  - Guru Nanak's teachings called for the **welfare** of all people, especially the oppressed, advocating for social justice, equality, and the removal of exploitation.

- **Humanitarian Values**:

  - He taught the importance of **selfless service** (seva) and **sharing** (vand chakna), encouraging his followers to serve humanity and help those in need.

- **Spiritual Unity**:

  - Guru Nanak emphasized the **unity of all religions**, teaching that all paths leading to God are valid, whether Hindu, Muslim, or otherwise, as long as they are based on truth and love.

- **Rejecting Asceticism**:

  - Unlike some religious traditions, Guru Nanak rejected asceticism and promoted a balanced life, where one could be engaged in the world while staying spiritually connected to God.

- **Foundation of Sikhism**:

  - Guru Nanak laid the foundation of **Sikhism**, which emphasized **devotion to one God**, the importance of **community (Sangat)**, and the **Guru's teachings** as the guiding light

Ans – 5.)

- **Alvars**:

- The **Alvars** were Tamil poet-saints devoted to **Vishnu**, who lived between the 6th and 9th centuries CE.

- Their hymns emphasized **devotion (bhakti)** to Vishnu and criticized ritualism, highlighting personal devotion as the path to salvation.

- They established a **strong relationship with the state** by their influence on the religious and social landscape, especially in the Tamil region, and their hymns were patronized by local kings

- **Nayanars**:

- The **Nayanars** were Tamil poet-saints dedicated to **Shiva**, also active between the 6th and 9th centuries CE.

- They expressed deep devotion through their hymns, focusing on **the grace of Shiva** and the rejection of caste distinctions, advocating for a more inclusive approach to spirituality.

- They were **closely connected to the states** through their patronage by local rulers, who supported their temples and helped spread Shaivism

- **Connection with States**:

- Both **Alvars** and **Nayanars** were instrumental in the spread of **bhakti** movements, which resonated with rulers who sought to **legitimize their power** through religious authority.

- **Kings** often patronized the temples of Vishnu and Shiva built by these saints, solidifying their role in state-building by associating their reigns with divine support and religious legitimacy

Ans – 6.)

Sufis: were Muslim mystics who sought a direct, personal experience of **God** through **intense devotion**, **prayer**, and **meditation**.

- They emphasized **inner purity**, **love**, and **self-discipline** and were known for their practices like **dhikr** (remembrance of God) and **sama** (spiritual music and dance)

Causes of Growth of Sufism –

- **Spread of Islam**: As Islam spread across South Asia, Sufism helped in **adapting** Islamic teachings to local traditions and made the religion more accessible to people, especially through its emphasis on **personal devotion**.

- **Social and Cultural Harmony**: Sufism was seen as a bridge between **Islam** and local cultural traditions, promoting a message of **universal love** and tolerance, especially in a diverse and pluralistic society.

- **Rejection of Ritualism**: Sufism's focus on **inner spirituality** appealed to many who found the rigid formalism of orthodox Islam to be inaccessible or alienating

Relation with the State:

- **Patronage**: Sufis enjoyed the **patronage** of various rulers who saw them as religious figures capable of providing divine legitimacy to their rule.

- **Influence on the masses**: Sufis played a role in spreading Islam and were often consulted by rulers for their **spiritual advice** and **political influence**.

- **Social Role**: Sufi saints often had large followings among the common people, transcending religious divisions and helping **states** consolidate their rule by creating a **bond between the rulers and the ruled** through religious harmony

Ans – 7.) Answer would be same as Answer no. 4 (Bhakti and sufi traditions)

Ans - 8.)

- **Women in Alvar and Nayanar Traditions**: Women like **Andal** and **Karaikkal Ammaiyar** played a significant role in the **Alvar and Nayanar traditions**, challenging patriarchal norms through their devotion and compositions.

- **Andal's Compositions**: **Andal**, a woman Alvar, saw herself as the beloved of Vishnu, and her **devotional verses** continue to be widely sung, reflecting her intense love for the deity.

- **Karaikkal Ammaiyar's Asceticism**: **Karaikkal Ammaiyar**, a Shiva devotee, embraced **extreme asceticism** to achieve her spiritual goal, and her **compositions** were preserved within the Nayanar tradition.

- **Challenge to Patriarchal Norms**: These women **renounced social roles**, yet did not join religious orders, making their **spiritual independence** a direct challenge to societal expectations

Ans – 9.)

- **Monotheism**: Islam emphasizes **belief in one God (Allah)**, and the ultimate goal is to submit to His will.

- **Prophethood**: Muslims believe in **prophets** as messengers of God, with **Prophet Muhammad** being the final messenger.

- **Five Pillars**: The foundation of Islam is based on the **Five Pillars**, which include **faith, prayer, fasting, charity, and pilgrimage** to Mecca.

- **Equality**: Islam promotes **equality** and the idea that all people are equal before Allah, irrespective of their social status.

- **Submission to Divine Will**: The central philosophy of Islam is to **submit to the will of Allah**, leading a life in accordance with His guidance and teachings.

- **The Quran**: The **Quran** is the holy book of Islam, believed to be the literal word of God, providing guidance on all aspects of life

Ans – 10.)

- **Divine Love**: Sufism emphasizes **love for God (Allah)** as the core of spiritual practice, seeking union with the Divine through intense devotion.

- **Inner Purity**: Sufis believe in purifying the **inner self** (heart and soul) to experience direct communion with God.

- **Spiritual Practice**: Practices like **dhikr** (remembrance of God), **recitation**, and **whirling** (as seen in the Mevlevi order) are central to attaining spiritual enlightenment.

- **Renunciation**: Sufism advocates **renunciation of worldly attachments**, focusing on humility, simplicity, and asceticism to strengthen one's connection to God.

- **Universal Brotherhood**: Sufism promotes the idea of **universal love and equality**, transcending social distinctions like caste and creed.

- **Mystical Experience**: Sufis believe in the **direct mystical experience** of God's presence

- **Poetry and Music**: Sufi poetry (like that of **Rumi**) and **music** play an important role in expressing divine love and the longing for union with God

Ans – 11.) Answer would be same as Answer no. 5 (Bhakti and sufi traditions)

Ans - 12.)

- **Shaikh Nizamuddin Auliya** was a prominent **Sufi saint** of the **Chishti Order** in India, known for spiritual teachings and practices.

- He emphasized **love, devotion, and service** to humanity as central to spiritual progress.

- Nizamuddin Auliya was known for his **simple and compassionate lifestyle**, attracting many followers through his humility.

- His **dargah** (tomb) in **Delhi** remains a major site of **pilgrimage**, symbolizing influence on Sufism iIndia.

- He believed in **helping the poor and the needy**, and his **musical gatherings** (sama) were meant to inspire spiritual devotion through music and poetry.

- Nizamuddin Auliya's teachings promoted **peace, tolerance**, **unity among all religions**

Ans – 13.)

- The **Chishti order** celebrated their devotionalism through **music and poetry**, particularly **qawwali**, which was used to express love and devotion to God.

- They also practiced **asceticism** and **service to the community**, focusing on helping the poor and marginalized.

- **Sufi saints** of the Chishti order often held **weekly gatherings** (majlis) where **spiritual talks** and **recitations** of poetry took place.

- **Worship** in the Chishti tradition was marked by a deep **emotional connection** to God, with a focus on inner purification and **surrender to divine will**.

- **Dargahs** (shrines) of Chishti saints became important centers of spiritual life, where **devotees** expressed their devotion and sought blessings

Ans – 14.) • **Khanqah** is a **Sufi lodge** or **center** where Sufi saints and their disciples gathered for spiritual practices, learning, and communal activities.

• It served as a **place for meditation**, **prayer**, and **guidance**, fostering a sense of community among followers.

• The **Khanqah** was a place of **hospitality** where the poor and travelers were provided food and shelter.

• It played a significant role in the **dissemination of Sufi teachings**, often through **poetry, music**, and **spiritual discourse**.

• **Khanqahs** became **important centers of social welfare** and cultural exchange in medieval India.

• The head of the Khanqah was often referred to as a **Sufi master**, providing spiritual guidance to the disciples

Ans – 15.) • **Qawwali**: A popular form of **Sufi devotional music**, expressing deep spiritual emotions and love for God. **Examples**: Works by **Amir Khusrau** and other Chishti saints.

• **Hymns and Bhajans**: The **Bhakti movement** inspired **devotional songs** in local languages that focused on **personal devotion** to God. **Examples**: Compositions of **Kabir**, **Mirabai**, and **Tulsidas**.

• **Dohe**: Short **couplets** used by **Bhakti poets** like **Kabir** to convey moral and spiritual lessons, focusing on inner devotion and social reform.

• **Vachanas**: **Spiritual poems** composed by **Basava** and **Lingayat saints**, conveying intense personal devotion and critique of ritualistic practices.

• **Sufi Poetry**: Focused on **love for God** and **divine union**, as seen in the works of **Rumi, Hafiz**, and **Ibn Arabi**.

• **Silsilas**: Poetic works associated with the **Sufi orders**, such as the **Chishti** and **Suhrawardi** traditions, emphasizing **spiritual practice** and **union with the divine**

Note – The Remaining questions are for your practice, hence their solutions aren't provided, Keep Practicing..!

Chapter – 7 (An Imperial Capital : Vijayanagara)

Ans – 1.)

- **Extensive Wall Systems**: The capital city, Hampi, had a series of strong defensive walls, gates, and bastions, which stretched over 80 kilometers, protecting the city from external invasions.

- **Strategic Location**: The city was surrounded by natural features such as hills and rivers, which enhanced its defenses, making it difficult for enemies to launch successful attacks.

- **Multiple Layers of Defense**: The city had several layers of fortifications, with different gates and walls for inner and outer defense, strengthening its ability to withstand sieges.

- **Architectural Integration**: The fortifications were integrated with the city's layout, including military structures, temples, and royal palaces, highlighting a well-planned defense strategy.

- **Innovative Gate Design**: Some gates, such as the famous "Elephant Stables" gate, were designed to accommodate war elephants, further emphasizing the military importance of the fortifications.

- **Symbol of Power**: The scale and complexity of the fortifications reflected the grandeur and military strength of the Vijayanagara Empire, serving both as a defense mechanism and a symbol of imperial authority

Ans – 2.)

- **Pioneering Surveyor**: Colin Mackenzie was the first Surveyor General of India, and his surveys marked the beginning of systematic documentation of India's historical sites, including Vijayanagara.

- **Extensive Documentation**: He collected detailed information on Vijayanagara through surveys, inscriptions, sketches, and oral traditions, contributing significantly to the reconstruction of its history.

- **Discovery of Hampi**: Mackenzie brought the ruins of Hampi, the capital of Vijayanagara, to wider attention through his documentation.

- **Collection of Inscriptions**: He collected and preserved numerous inscriptions, which served as critical sources for understanding the political, economic, and cultural aspects of Vijayanagara.

- **Foundation for Future Research**: His work laid the groundwork for later historians and archaeologists to study Vijayanagara, enriching knowledge of South Indian history

Ans – 3.)

- **Ritual Significance**: The Mahanavami Dibba served as a prominent platform for royal ceremonies and rituals, particularly during the annual Mahanavami festival (Dasara).

- **Symbol of Royal Power**: It was a site where kings showcased their power, wealth, and devotion through grand processions, military parades, and cultural performances.

- **Military Displays**: Armies, horses, and elephants were paraded in front of the king, symbolizing the might and preparedness of the empire.

- **Audience for the King**: The elevated platform allowed the king to be seen by large gatherings of people, reinforcing his divine and political authority.

- **Cultural Performances**: Dancers, musicians, and theatrical performances added to the grandeur, blending religious devotion with cultural expression.

- **Architectural Grandeur**: The intricate carvings on the platform highlighted its importance and celebrated the empire's artistic achievements.

- **Religious Devotion**: The festival emphasized the king's role as a patron of religion and guardian of dharma, central to the empire's identity

Ans – 4.) Answer would be same as Answer no. 1 (An Imperial capital: Vijayanagara)

Ans – 5.)

- **Rama Raya's Dominance**: Rama Raya became the de facto ruler of Vijayanagara, exercising significant power and influence in state affairs.

- **Provoked Rivalries**: His aggressive policies and interference in the politics of the Deccan Sultanates created animosities among them.

- **Battle of Talikota**: In 1565, his alliances with certain sultanates backfired, leading to a coalition of Sultanates (Bijapur, Golconda, Ahmednagar, and Bidar) against Vijayanagara.

- **Defeat at Talikota**: Rama Raya was killed during the Battle of Talikota, resulting in a catastrophic defeat for Vijayanagara.

- **City's Destruction**: After the battle, the victorious Sultanates plundered and destroyed Vijayanagara, marking the empire's decline.

- **Legacy of Mismanagement**: His policies, while aimed at maintaining dominance, ultimately led to the empire's vulnerability and downfall

Ans – 6.)

- **Religious Importance**: The Virupaksha temple was dedicated to Lord Shiva, worshipped as Virupaksha, and was a prominent religious center in the Vijayanagara Empire.

- **Patronized by Rulers**: The temple received royal patronage and became a symbol of the empire's devotion to Shaivism.

- **Continuous Worship**: Unlike many other temples, it has remained a functional temple, continuing rituals from the Vijayanagara period to the present.

- **Architectural Excellence**: The temple showcased the Dravidian architectural style with intricate carvings, a tall gopuram (gateway), and a grand pillared hall.

- **Cultural Hub**: It was a center for cultural and religious activities, hosting festivals, rituals, and ceremonies.

- **Pilgrimage Site**: The temple attracted pilgrims from across the region, highlighting its significance in the religious landscape of South India.

- **Association with Hampi**: Located in Hampi, the capital of Vijayanagara, it stood as a spiritual and architectural landmark of the empire

Ans – 7.)

- **Extravagant Architecture**: The Vithala temple is known for its grand and intricate Dravidian architectural style, reflecting the pinnacle of Vijayanagara art.

- **Stone Chariot**: A remarkable feature of the temple is the iconic stone chariot, symbolizing the architectural innovation and craftsmanship of the Vijayanagara period.

- **Musical Pillars**: The temple has intricately carved musical pillars that emit different tones when struck, showcasing the advanced understanding of acoustics by the artisans.

- **Sprawling Complex**: The temple is part of a vast complex with numerous halls, sanctums, and pavilions, indicating its significance as a major religious and cultural hub.

- **Cultural Fusion**: Its carvings and sculptures represent a blend of Hindu mythology, cultural themes, and artistic creativity.

- **Unfinished Gopuram**: The temple's incomplete gopuram (tower) highlights the challenges faced during its construction, adding to its historical intrigue.

- **World Heritage Recognition**: As part of the Hampi UNESCO World Heritage Site, the Vithala temple represents the zenith of Vijayanagara Empire's architectural legacy.

Ans -8.)

- **Role of Rayas**: The Rayas were the kings of the Vijayanagara Empire who provided centralized leadership and ruled over the empire, ensuring stability and expansion.

- **Political Authority**: The Rayas maintained control over the central administration and coordinated various aspects of governance, including military campaigns and trade policies.

- **Role of Nayakas**: The Nayakas were military chiefs and governors appointed by the Rayas to administer specific regions or territories within the empire.

- **Military Contributions**: Nayakas were responsible for maintaining regional armies and supporting the Rayas during wars and military expeditions.

- **Revenue Collection**: Nayakas collected taxes from their regions and contributed a portion to the central treasury, ensuring economic stability.

- **Autonomy of Nayakas**: While serving the central authority, Nayakas enjoyed considerable autonomy in managing their territories.

- **Rayas-Nayakas Relations**: The relationship between the Rayas and Nayakas was mutually dependent, but tensions occasionally arose, particularly as Nayakas grew powerful over time.

- **Decline of Empire**: Disputes between the Rayas and the increasingly assertive Nayakas contributed to the weakening and eventual decline of the Vijayanagara Empire

Ans – 9.)

Apogee of Vijayanagara Empire –

- **Founding and Consolidation**: Established in 1336 by Harihara and Bukka, the empire unified South India and expanded rapidly.

- **Strong Administration**: The Rayas centralized governance and established a structured administrative system.

- **Military Strength**: Vijayanagara maintained a powerful army and naval presence to defend and expand its territories.

- **Economic Prosperity**: The empire controlled lucrative trade routes and fostered agricultural and commercial growth.

- **Cultural Flourishing**: Supported temple architecture, art, and literature, with landmarks like the Virupaksha and Vithala temples.

Decline of Vijayanagara Empire –

- **Weakened Leadership**: The defeat of Rama Raya in the Battle of Talikota (1565) marked the empire's decline.

- **Battle of Talikota**: A coalition of Deccan sultanates decisively defeated Vijayanagara forces, leading to massive destruction.

- **Nayaka Assertion**: The Nayakas, previously loyal to the central authority, began asserting independence.

- **Loss of Trade**: Decline in overseas trade due to political instability further weakened the economy.

- **Shift in Power**: Regional powers rose as the centralized structure of Vijayanagara disintegrated

Ans -10.)

- **eparate from Urban Spaces**: The royal centre was distinct from the rest of the city, emphasizing its exclusivity and importance

- **Fortified Enclosure**: Surrounded by fortifications to protect the rulers and administrative elite

- **Royal Structures**: Included the king's palace, audience hall, and the Mahanavami Dibba, showcasing grandeur and political authority.

- **Religious and Ceremonial Buildings**: Temples within the royal centre reflected the king's divine association, like the Hazara Rama temple.

- **Waterworks**: Advanced irrigation systems, such as aqueducts and reservoirs, demonstrated engineering expertise.

- **Granaries and Stables**: Structures like granaries and elephant stables indicated self-sufficiency and military preparedness.

- **Administrative Hub**: Served as the centre of governance, where royal decrees and diplomatic meetings occurred.

- **Strategic Layout**: Designed to reflect the power, wealth, and divinity of the Vijayanagara rulers while ensuring functionality

Ans – 11.)

- **Expansion of Territory**: Krishnadeva Raya acquired the Raichur Doab (1512) and subdued Odisha rulers (1514).

- **Military Success**: Defeated the Sultan of Bijapur decisively in 1520.

- **State of Vigilance**: Maintained military readiness alongside peace and prosperity.

- **Architectural Legacy**: Built fine temples and added gopurams to major South Indian temples.

- **Urban Development**: Established Nagalapuram in honor of his mother.

- **Historical Descriptions**: Vijayanagara's detailed accounts are from his reign or soon after

Ans – 12.)

- **Introduction of Amara Nayaka System**: A system where local military leaders, called Amara Nayakas, governed regions on behalf of the king.

- **Decentralization**: Allowed for efficient administration and control over vast territories by empowering regional commanders.

- **Military and Revenue Roles**: Amara Nayakas were responsible for maintaining troops, collecting taxes, and ensuring law and order.

- **Feudal Structure**: Strengthened the feudal structure, with regional leaders directly loyal to the king.

- **Consolidation of Power**: Enabled the Vijayanagara Empire to manage a large and diverse empire effectively through regional autonomy

Ans – 13.)

- **Rivers**: The empire was strategically located between the Tungabhadra and Krishna rivers, which provided vital water resources

- **Reservoirs**: Large reservoirs were constructed to store water for irrigation and drinking

- **Canals**: An extensive network of canals was built to irrigate agricultural lands – Hiriya Canal

- **Tanks**: Numerous tanks and ponds were created for rainwater harvesting and irrigation – Kamalapuram Tank

- **Stepwells**: The construction of stepwells ensured a steady supply of water, particularly in arid region

Ans – 14.)

Lotus Mahal - unique example of Indo-Islamic architecture in the Vijayanagara Empire.

- It is a two-storied pavilion, shaped like a lotus flower, and believed to have been used by the royal women of the empire.

- The structure blends Hindu and Islamic architectural styles, showcasing intricate arches and domes

Audience Hall - was an essential structure for royal functions and public meetings.

* distinguished by its large platform and pillars, where the king would meet with his ministers, officials, and dignitaries.

* It symbolized the power and grandeur of the Vijayanagara court

Mahanavami Dibba - was a ceremonial platform used during the Mahanavami festival, a significant occasion in the Vijayanagara Empire.

* The platform was richly decorated and used for royal rituals and celebrations.

* It is a monumental structure that reflects the grandeur and religious significance of the empire

Hazara Rama Temple - dedicated to Lord Rama and is famous for its intricate carvings that depict scenes from the Ramayana.

* Located in the royal center of Vijayanagara, it was likely a private temple for the royal family.

* The temple features beautiful stone carvings and murals, showcasing the artistic excellence of the period

Note – The Remaining questions are for your practice, hence their solutions aren't provided, Keep Practicing..!

Chapter – 8 (Peasants, Zamindars and the State)

Ans – 1.)

- **Land Revenue as Economic Mainstay**:

  - The Mughal empire's primary source of income was land revenue, which funded its military and administrative systems.

- **Zamindari System**:

  - The Zamindars acted as intermediaries, collecting land revenue from peasants and passing it on to the state, ensuring a steady revenue stream.

- **Ain-i-Akbari**:

  - Emperor Akbar's land revenue system, detailed in the Ain-i-Akbari, classified land into categories for efficient tax collection, further strengthening the economy.

- **Crop-based Taxation**:

  - Revenue was largely based on the productivity of land, with peasants paying a portion of their crops, usually one-third, as tax.

- **Land Revenue Reforms**:

  - Akbar's reforms, like the introduction of the **Zabt system**, standardized revenue collection, improving state finances and agricultural output.

- **Agricultural Focus**:

  - The empire invested in agriculture, promoting irrigation and land reclamation, leading to increased productivity and greater revenue from land.

- **Economic Growth and Stability**:

  - Stable revenue from land taxation allowed the Mughal empire to maintain a strong military, foster trade, and ensure prosperity across the empire

Ans – 2.) • Local Governance:

- Panchayats played a key role in local governance, managing disputes and regulating social and economic affairs at the village level in Mughal rural society.

• Community Decision-Making:

- Panchayats were composed of village elders and leaders who resolved conflicts, ensuring social harmony and maintaining traditional customs.

• Revenue Collection:

- The Panchayat helped in collecting land revenue from peasants, acting as intermediaries between the peasants and the Zamindars or the state.

• Agricultural Management:

- The Panchayat facilitated agricultural practices, including the distribution of water resources and land, ensuring the smooth functioning of rural economy.

• Social Control:

- Panchayats were responsible for enforcing local customs and traditions, maintaining order, and ensuring that peasants adhered to societal norms.

• Limited State Involvement:

- In rural areas, the Mughal state relied on Panchayats to manage day-to-day matters, reducing the need for direct intervention in village affairs

Ans – 3.)

• evenue Collectors:

- Zamindars were primarily responsible for collecting land revenue from peasants on behalf of the Mughal state.

• Intermediaries:

- They acted as intermediaries between the Mughal administration and rural society, transmitting the state's revenue demands to the local level.

- **Landowners**:

    - Zamindars often owned large tracts of land, with peasants working under them, and they derived significant income from their land holdings.

- **Maintaining Order**:

    - They were also responsible for maintaining law and order in their territories, including managing disputes among peasants.

- **Military Support**:

    - Some Zamindars provided military support to the Mughal rulers, either through personal troops or resources, in times of conflict.

- **Patrons of Local Culture**:

    - Many Zamindars were patrons of local culture and arts, supporting temples, schools, and artisans within their regions.

- **Enforcement of State Policies**:

    - They played a crucial role in enforcing Mughal state policies and ensuring peasants met their revenue obligations

Ans – 4.)

- **Labor Force**:

    - Women were an essential part of the agrarian labor force, contributing to farming activities such as sowing, harvesting, and processing crops.

- **Household Management**:

    - They played a key role in managing household tasks, including the care of animals, food preparation, and maintaining domestic resources.

- **Reproductive Role**:

    - Women's reproductive role ensured the continuation of the workforce, with childbirth contributing to the labor pool for future generations.

- **Economic Contribution**:

  - Women's work in textile production, weaving, and other cottage industries contributed to the local economy, making them vital to agrarian prosperity.

- **Social Stability**:

  - Women's ability to manage domestic and agricultural responsibilities helped maintain social and economic stability within agrarian communities

Ans – 5.)

- **Detailed Revenue System**:

  - *Ain-i-Akbari* provides insights into the revenue system, detailing the assessment and collection of land taxes during Akbar's reign.

- **Land Classification**:

  - It outlines the different types of land and their productivity, offering a detailed classification of agricultural lands based on fertility.

- **Role of Zamindars**:

  - The document highlights the role of zamindars in managing land and collecting taxes, reflecting their power and influence in the agrarian economy.

- **Peasant Life**:

  - It sheds light on the lives of peasants, their obligations to landowners, and the resources available to them in rural society.

- **Agrarian Economy**:

  - *Ain-i-Akbari* serves as a key source for understanding the economic framework of the Mughal Empire, particularly the land revenue policies and agricultural practices

Ans – 6.)

- **Khud-Kashta**:

  - Residents of the village where they held land.
  - Cultivated their own land in their home village.

- **Pahi-Kashta**:

  - Non-resident cultivators who worked land in a different village.
  - Could be voluntary, seeking better revenue terms elsewhere.
  - Could also be involuntary, driven by economic hardship or famine.

Ans – 7.) • **Factors for Agricultural Expansion**:

  - Abundance of land, available labor, and the mobility of peasants led to constant agricultural expansion.

- **Primary Crops**:

  - Basic staples like rice, wheat, and millets were the most commonly cultivated crops.
  - Rice was grown in areas with over 40 inches of rainfall, followed by wheat and millets in drier regions.

- **Role of Monsoons**:

  - Monsoons were crucial for Indian agriculture, providing the necessary rainfall.
  - Crops requiring extra water relied on artificial irrigation systems.

- **Irrigation Projects**:

  - The state supported irrigation projects, such as new canal constructions and repairs of old ones (e.g., the **shahnahr** in Punjab during Shah Jahan's reign).

- **Technologies in Agriculture**:

  - Labour-intensive agriculture used technologies like wooden ploughs with iron tips, which helped preserve moisture.
  - Seed planting was done with a drill pulled by oxen, though broadcasting seeds was more common.
  - Hoeing and weeding were done using a narrow iron blade with a wooden handle

Ans – 8.)

- **Caste-based Inequality**:

  - Mughal society had deep-rooted caste distinctions, where social hierarchy determined individuals' rights and opportunities.

- **Role of Brahmins**:

  - Brahmins held privileged positions, especially in religious, administrative, and land-owning roles, contributing to the inequality.

- **Untouchability**:

  - Lower caste groups, including untouchables, faced social exclusion and were often relegated to menial tasks, with limited rights or access to resources.

- **Zamindars and Caste**:

  - While zamindars were often upper-caste, lower-caste peasants had little power over land and were subjugated by the zamindar's authority.

- **Jat and Rajput Roles**:

  - Jats and Rajputs, considered higher castes, were significant in the military and political spheres, highlighting the hierarchical society structure

Ans – 9.)

- **Jati Panchayats**:

  - Jati Panchayats were village councils made up of prominent members of a particular caste (jati) in Mughal society.

- **Role in Dispute Resolution**:

  - They were responsible for resolving disputes within their community, including issues related to marriage, land, and social conduct.

- **Authority and Influence**: The Panchayats had significant local power, sometimes overriding the authority of the state or other external rulers in certain matters.

- **Caste-Based Justice**:

  - Their decisions were based on caste customs and norms, enforcing social and economic rules within the community.

- **Regulation of Social Life**:

  - Jati Panchayats helped maintain order and cohesion within the village, ensuring that caste hierarchies were respected and preserved

Ans – 10.)

- **Exchange between Producers**:

  - Villages had a complex system of exchange between producers, with artisans and peasants interacting frequently.

- **Artisans in Village Society**:

  - In some villages, artisans made up to 25% of households, and the distinction between artisans and peasants was often fluid.

- **Artisan Tasks**:

  - Many cultivators also engaged in crafts like dyeing, textile printing, pottery-making, and agricultural tool repairs during off-peak agricultural seasons.

- **Services and Compensation**:

  - Village artisans provided specialized services and were compensated in various ways, often through shares of the harvest or land allotments.

- **Miras/Watan System**:

  - In Maharashtra, artisans received land, known as miras or watan, as hereditary holdings in exchange for their services.

- **Mutual Negotiation and Jajmani System**:

  - Artisans and peasants often negotiated remuneration for services, such as zamindars paying blacksmiths and carpenters in daily allowances or goods, a system later referred to as the jajmani system.

Ans – 11.) Answer would be similar to Answer no. 4 (Peasants, Zamindars and the State)

Ans – 12.)

- **Pastoralism**:

  - Many communities practiced pastoralism, herding cattle, sheep, and goats in regions unsuitable for cultivation.

- **Shifting Agriculture**:

  - In hilly and forested areas, some communities practiced shifting cultivation, clearing forests and farming for a few seasons before moving.

- **Forest Produce**:

  - Tribes and forest-dwellers gathered and traded forest products like honey, beeswax, and medicinal herbs.

- **Fishing and Hunting**:

  - Coastal and riverine communities engaged in fishing, while some forest tribes relied on hunting as a livelihood.

- **Craft and Artisanal Work**:

  - Many rural households supplemented their income with crafts, weaving, and pottery, particularly during the agricultural off-season.

- **Nomadic Trades**:

  - Nomadic groups traded goods such as salt, grain, and other necessities, connecting rural areas to broader markets.

- **Integration of Diverse Livelihoods**:

  - Rural India was a mix of sedentary agriculture, artisanal activities, and non-agricultural pursuits, reflecting a diverse economic landscape

Ans – 13.)

- **Meaning of "Jangli"**:

    - The term "jangli" referred to forest dwellers whose livelihood depended on forest activities, not a lack of "civilization."

- **Livelihood Activities**:

Forest dwellers engaged in seasonal activities :-

- **Spring**: Collecting forest produce.

- **Summer**: Fishing.

- **Monsoon**: Cultivation.

- **Autumn/Winter**: Hunting

- **Mobility** - was central to their way of life, enabling them to adapt to seasonal livelihoods.

- **State's Perception** - forest was seen subversive space offering refuge to rebels and tax evaders.

- **Babur's View** - jungles provided natural defenses for rebellious groups, making tax collection difficult

Note – The Remaining questions are for your practice, hence their solutions aren't provided, Keep Practicing..!

Chapter – 9 (Colonialism and the Countryside)

Ans – 1.)

- **Territorial Encroachment**: The Santhals settled in the Damin-i-Koh area under British encouragement, encroaching on Paharia land.

- **Agricultural Expansion**: Santhals cleared forests for cultivation, threatening the traditional forest-based economy of the Paharias.

- **Cultural Differences**: Distinct lifestyles and practices led to tensions, with the Paharias relying on hunting and gathering and the Santhals practicing settled agriculture.

- **Economic Disruption**: The Paharias faced reduced access to forest resources due to the increasing Santhal population and farming activities.

- **British Interference**: The British favored Santhal settlement for revenue generation, undermining Paharia autonomy and fostering conflict

Ans – 2.)

- **Objective of the Report**: The Fifth Report (1813) was presented to the British Parliament to review the administrative and economic performance of the East India Company.

- **Focus on Land Revenue**: Highlighted issues related to the Permanent Settlement in Bengal, especially the exploitation of peasants by zamindars.

- **Criticism of Company Policies**: Criticized the Company's monopoly over trade and its governance practices, including neglect of welfare.

- **Bias in Reporting**: Written by British officials, the report reflected colonial interests, often emphasizing the need for tighter control over India.

- **Role of Indigenous Society**: Offered a detailed, though skewed, account of Indian society, economy, and landholding patterns.

- **Impact on Policy**: Played a key role in shaping debates about colonial governance and led to increased intervention in local administration

Ans – 3.)

Factors Influencing Revenue settlement –

- **Revenue Maximization**: The British needed a stable and predictable income to fund their administrative and military expenditures.

- **Administrative Convenience**: Fixing revenue permanently reduced the burden of yearly settlements and eased governance.

- **Zamindar Support**: Aimed to create a loyal class of zamindars who would act as intermediaries between the British and the peasants.

- **Influence of British Economic Ideas**: Reflected contemporary notions of private property and capitalist agricultural production.

- **Urgency after Famine**: The Bengal famine of 1770 highlighted the need for a stable agrarian economy

Consequences –

- **Peasant Exploitation**: Zamindars extracted high rents from peasants, leading to widespread distress

- **Zamindar Indebtedness**: Many zamindars defaulted on payments and lost their lands to auctions

- **Commercialization of Agriculture**: Encouraged cash crops over subsistence farming, altering traditional agrarian practices.

- **Administrative Stability**: Provided the British with a predictable revenue but weakened their control over rural society.

- **Regional Disparities**: Benefited zamindars in some areas while worsening conditions for peasants in others

Ans -4.) Reasons for Jotedars' Rise to Power:

- **Large Landholdings**: Jotedars were rich peasants who controlled significant tracts of land.

- **Economic Strength**: They had surplus produce and capital, enabling them to lend money to smaller peasants.

- **Role in Agrarian Economy**: They often leased out land to under-tenants and collected rent.

- **Resistance to Zamindars**: Unlike dependent peasants, jotedars frequently resisted zamindars and their demands.

- **Local Influence**: They held significant social and political influence in rural communities.

Outcomes of Their Power:

- **Decline of Zamindari Authority**: Jotedars emerged as a competing class, weakening the zamindars' dominance.

- **Peasant Support**: Jotedars often supported smaller cultivators, consolidating their local power base.

- **Economic Autonomy**: They controlled agricultural production and contributed to rural trade networks.

- **Resistance Movements**: Jotedars played a key role in agrarian resistance against oppressive revenue systems

Ans – 5.)

- **Encouraged by Colonial Authorities**: British administrators encouraged the Santhals to settle as part of their policy to expand agricultural frontiers and bring wastelands under cultivation.

- **Land Clearance for Agriculture**: The Santhals cleared forests and brought the land into agricultural use, transforming the landscape.

- **Attraction of Daman-i-koh**: The British designated the area as Daman-i-koh and offered incentives such as land grants and low rents to attract Santhals.

- **Escape from Exploitation**: The Santhals, previously exploited by moneylenders, landlords, and officials in other regions, sought refuge in these new settlements.

- **Formation of Settled Villages**: The Santhals established settled villages with an agrarian lifestyle, cultivating rice, pulses, and other crops.

- **Economic Contribution**: Their settlements significantly boosted agricultural productivity in the Rajmahal hills' periphery, contributing to colonial revenue.

Ans – 6.)

- **Cotton Shortage**: The American Civil War disrupted cotton production in the United States, leading to a shortage of raw cotton in global markets, including India.

- **Increased Demand for Indian Cotton**: With American cotton unavailable, British textile mills increased their demand for Indian cotton, causing a rise in cotton prices.

- **High Prices and Exploitation**: Ryots (peasants) in India faced high prices for seeds, tools, and other essentials, but the prices for their cotton remained low, leading to exploitation.

- **Increased Tax Burden**: The British government increased taxes on cotton production to meet war-related expenses, adding to the financial burden of the ryots.

- **Agricultural Distress**: The increased pressure on cotton cultivation, combined with irregular monsoon patterns and the exploitative system of revenue collection, led to economic distress for the ryots

Ans – 7.)

- **Increased Land Revenue**: The Permanent Settlement of 1793 fixed high land revenue demands, burdening the zamindars, especially in times of poor harvests.

- **Economic Distress**: Fluctuations in crop yields due to irregular monsoons and famines caused economic hardship, making it difficult for zamindars to meet revenue targets.

- **Commercialization of Agriculture**: The focus on cash crops, such as indigo and cotton, led to a neglect of food crops, leaving zamindars vulnerable to market fluctuations and crop failure.

- **Exploitation by British Authorities**: The British officials and intermediaries extracted excessive revenue from zamindars without considering local conditions, worsening their financial situation.

- **Debt and Loans**: Zamindars increasingly relied on loans from moneylenders to pay revenue, plunging them into further debt when they could not repay the loans.

- **Weakening of Zamindari System**: As zamindars faced financial strain, their power and influence over peasants diminished, undermining the traditional agrarian structure

Ans – 8.)

- **Fixed Land Revenue**: Introduced in 1793, it fixed the land revenue at a specific amount to be paid by zamindars to the British, regardless of crop yield or economic conditions.

- **Zamindar Control**: Zamindars were made the hereditary landowners, responsible for collecting and remitting the revenue from peasants, but with limited power over land administration.

- **Exploitation of Peasants**: Zamindars were allowed to extract high rents from peasants, often leading to their exploitation and economic distress.

- **Loss of Traditional Rights**: The permanent settlement weakened the rights of local peasants by empowering zamindars and reducing the role of traditional village headmen and communities.

- **Economic Burden**: The fixed revenue system placed a heavy burden on zamindars, especially during years of poor harvests, leading to their inability to pay the set revenue.

- **Decline of Zamindars**: Over time, many zamindars, unable to meet the revenue demands, lost their lands and estates to moneylenders and the British, leading to the weakening of the zamindari system.

- **Lack of Agricultural Reforms**: The system did not encourage agricultural improvements or innovation, as the zamindars were focused on meeting the fixed revenue, often at the expense of long-term development

Ans – 9.) • **Demand from British Textile Mills**: The Industrial Revolution in Britain led to an increased demand for raw cotton, which was met by cotton produced in India, especially from Bombay Deccan.

- **American Civil War (1861-1865)**: The disruption of cotton supply from the American South due to the Civil War led to a surge in cotton exports from India, particularly from the Bombay region.

- **Infrastructure Development**: Improved transportation, including the construction of railways and better roads, facilitated the movement of cotton from rural areas to Bombay's port for export.

- **Expansion of Cultivation**: British colonial policies encouraged the expansion of cotton cultivation in the Deccan region to meet the growing demand for raw cotton.

- **Decline of Traditional Crops**: The colonial emphasis on cash crops led to a reduction in the cultivation of food crops, with cotton becoming a primary focus for many farmers.

- **British Monopoly on Trade**: The British controlled the cotton trade, both in terms of pricing and export, ensuring a steady demand for Indian cotton

Ans – 10.)

- **Revolt of Zamindars**: The Burdwan action was a response to the **resistance by the zamindars** (landlords) against the **revenue demands** under the Permanent Settlement system.

- **British Response**: The British authorities, led by the **East India Company**, responded with severe military action, attempting to quash the resistance and assert control over the zamindars.

- **Public Attention**: It attracted **public attention** as it involved a direct clash between the **local elite** (zamindars) and the British administration, symbolizing the deepening tensions under colonial rule.

- **Symbol of Resistance**: It became a **symbol of resistance** against the exploitative revenue system imposed by the British, stirring public discourse about colonial authority and its impact on local societies.

- **Outcome and Consequences**: The action resulted in the **defeat of the zamindars**, which marked a significant consolidation of British power in Bengal and further entrenchment of the Permanent Settlement

Ans – 11.)

- **Geographical and Administrative Differences**: Bengal's **unique agrarian structure** and **well-defined revenue systems** made it suitable for the Permanent Settlement, but other regions had different land tenure systems.

- **Resistance from Local Elites**: In regions like **South India** and **North India**, local rulers and zamindars resisted the imposition of the Permanent Settlement, as it undermined their traditional power and autonomy.

- **Economic Factors**: In other regions, **land productivity** and revenue generation were less predictable, making it difficult to implement a fixed revenue system without facing fiscal challenges.

- **Political Instability**: Many regions outside Bengal faced ongoing political instability, making it harder to enforce the system consistently, as seen in areas like **Awadh** or **Deccan**.

- **Differences in Agrarian Structure**: Other regions had a **larger number of smaller cultivators** or **different forms of tenancy**, which made the Permanent Settlement impractical for such diverse social structures

Ans -12.)

- **Exorbitant Interest Rates**: Moneylenders charged **high interest rates** that made it difficult for ryots to repay loans, leading to a cycle of indebtedness.

- **Exploitation**: Moneylenders often exploited ryots by taking advantage of their **desperation during bad harvests**, exacerbating their financial struggles.

- **Debt Traps**: Many ryots were forced to pledge their land as collateral, which **further entrenched them in debt** and sometimes led to the **loss of their land**.

- **Collaboration with Colonial Authorities**: Moneylenders often had **close ties with colonial officials**, which enabled them to **enforce harsh debt repayments** on ryots, deepening their resentment.

- **Perceived Deceit**: The ryots viewed moneylenders as **dishonest and manipulative**, as they often used **tricks** to deceive and entrap them in unmanageable debt

Ans – 13.)

- **Time-Barred Debts**: It stipulated that **debts** could only be claimed within a specific time frame (typically 12 years). After this period, the debt was considered **irrecoverable** by law

- **Limitations on Ryots**: The law became a symbol of **oppression against ryots** because it **disadvantaged them** in disputes with moneylenders. Many ryots were unaware of this law or unable to defend themselves against moneylenders who used it to their advantage.

- **Moneylender Advantage**: Moneylenders exploited the law to **foreclose on ryots' lands** by manipulating the legal system, forcing ryots into debt even after the legal time for claims had passed.

- **Inequity**: The law often worked in **favor of wealthy moneylenders** and colonial authorities while **disempowering poor ryots**, reinforcing social and economic inequality

Ans – 14.)

The revenue system introduced in the **Bombay Deccan** was the **Ryotwari System**, main features were –

- **Direct Taxation**: Land revenue was **collected directly from the ryots (peasants)** rather than through intermediaries like zamindars.

- **Individual Assessment**: Land was assessed and taxed on the basis of **individual plots** and the crops grown, with the amount of tax fixed for each ryot.

- **Permanent Fixation**: The revenue was often **fixed permanently** or for a long term, though it was subject to review.

- **Responsibility of the Ryot**: The responsibility of paying the revenue was directly placed on the **peasant** (ryot), making them liable for any arrears.

- **Flexibility**: In contrast to the zamindari system, the Ryotwari system allowed for more **flexibility in land management**, but it also led to increased pressure on peasants to pay the taxes

Ans – 15.) • **Land as a Scarce Resource**: Ricardo's theory emphasized that land, being a **scarce resource**, had value based on its productivity and location

- **Rent Based on Fertility**: Landowners were entitled to a **rent** based on the fertility of their land, and more fertile land would attract higher rents.

- **Application in Bombay Deccan**: In the **Bombay Deccan**, the British applied this theory to assess the **value of land**, and the **revenue demand** was fixed accordingly, often burdening the peasants.

- **Land Revenue System**: The **Ryotwari System** in the Deccan was influenced by Ricardo's principles, where land was assessed based on its potential productivity, and rent/revenue was calculated accordingly, often disadvantaging the ryots

Ans – 16.) • **Loss of Financial Support**: Without loans, ryots could not afford the necessary inputs like **seeds, fertilizers, and tools** for cultivation, leading to poor agricultural productivity.

- **Increased Dependence on Moneylenders**: As the official credit system was inadequate, ryots had to turn to moneylenders for survival, often leading to **exorbitant interest rates**.

- **Debt Trap**: Unable to repay loans, many ryots became trapped in a cycle of debt, with the **moneylenders** taking possession of their land and property.

- **Rural Unrest**: The inability to access loans and the resultant exploitation by moneylenders contributed to **resentment and unrest** among the peasant class, fueling peasant movements.

- **Economic Hardship**: The refusal of loans pushed many ryots further into **economic distress**, undermining their ability to sustain their livelihoods and worsening poverty.

Note – The Remaining questions are for your practice, hence their solutions aren't provided, Keep Practicing..!

Chapter – 10 (Rebels and the Raj)\

Ans – 1.)

- **Political Instability**: The British annexation of Awadh in 1856, following the deposition of Nawab Wajid Ali Shah, caused resentment among the local rulers, nobility, and common people.

- **Economic Exploitation**: The annexation led to heavy taxation, economic distress, and the loss of livelihoods for peasants, zamindars, and soldiers.

- **Cultural and Religious Factors**: The British interference in local customs, including religious practices, aggravated tensions. The recruitment of sepoys from Awadh added to the anger.

- **Military Grievances**: The mutiny was further fueled by the Indian soldiers' (sepoys) discontent with British policies, particularly the use of the Enfield rifle and its rumored greased cartridges, which offended religious sentiments.

- **Local Leadership**: Leaders like Begum Hazrat Mahal and Nawab Khan fought against the British, drawing widespread support for the rebellion

Ans – 2.)

- **Appeal for Social Unity**: Rebel proclamations called for the unity of all castes, communities, and religions to fight against British rule, transcending traditional social divisions.

- **Economic and Political Freedom**: The proclamations promised the restoration of rights, privileges, and the protection of land and property from exploitation by the British.

- **Religious Tolerance**: Leaders like Bahadur Shah Zafar and Begum Hazrat Mahal emphasized unity among Hindus and Muslims, appealing to religious sentiments while opposing British attempts to divide communities.

- **Restoration of Traditional Leadership**: The rebels sought to reinstate traditional rulers and dismantle the British-imposed system, thus appealing to both the nobility and common people.

- **Nationalism**: The appeal for unity reflected a growing sense of national identity, aiming to overthrow foreign rule and restore India's sovereignty

Ans – 3.)

- **Literary Works**: Writers and poets, wrote about the revolt, preserving its events and sentiments in poetry and prose, which became a means of remembering the struggle.

- **Patriotic Poems**: Poems and songs became powerful tools to inspire national pride and kept the memory of the heroes of 1857 alive among the people.

- **Symbolic Art**: Paintings and illustrations were created to glorify the heroes of the revolt, depicting their bravery and sacrifice.

- **Historical Narratives**: Historical accounts and books written after the revolt aimed to document the struggle and its significance, influencing future generations' understanding of the event.

- **Nationalist Literature**: Writers and poets in later years used literature to critique British rule and highlight the events of 1857, thereby shaping nationalist discourse.

- **Public Memorials**: Statues and monuments were erected in memory of the leaders and warriors of the revolt, making the historical event tangible and visible to future generations.

- **Oral Tradition**: Folk songs and stories, passed down orally, celebrated the revolt's heroes and preserved the collective memory of resistance against British colonialism

Ans – 4.)

- **Strategic Location**: Awadh was geographically significant, situated in the heart of northern India, making it a key area for controlling the region.

- **Economic Importance**: The fertile land and agricultural productivity of Awadh made it an important source of revenue for the British.

- **Political Control**: By annexing Awadh, the British could strengthen their control over the entire northern plains, preventing any opposition to their rule.

- **Military Significance**: The region's proximity to Delhi and the northern frontiers made it crucial for British military strategy.

- **Resource Wealth**: Awadh was rich in resources like cotton and indigo, which were essential to the British economy, especially for the textile industry.

- **Threat of Rebellion**: The British feared that the independent and influential rulers of Awadh, particularly the Nawab, could support resistance against British rule, especially after the rising tension of 1857

Ans – 5.)

- **Spread of Fear**: Rumors of British atrocities, such as the use of cow and pig fat in cartridges, fueled anger and fear among the Indian soldiers and general public.

- **Mobilization of Discontent**: The rumors united people across regions, causing widespread resentment and fear, leading them to believe that their religious and cultural identities were under threat.

- **Reinforcement of Religious Sentiments**: Rumors about the British disrespecting Hindu and Muslim religious practices intensified communal tensions, rallying people to fight for their beliefs.

- **Rapid Spread of the Rebellion**: Rumors spread quickly, facilitating the spread of the revolt from one area to another, creating a sense of urgency among people to act.

- **Psychological Impact**: The rumors amplified the sense of injustice and oppression, prompting people to take action without knowing the full truth, but driven by the fear of losing their rights

Ans – 6.)

- **Reluctant Involvement**: Bahadur Shah Zafar initially hesitated to support the rebellion, but the growing unrest and calls for leadership from the rebels pressured him to take a stand.

- **Symbol of Unity**: As the Mughal Emperor, he was seen as a symbolic figurehead, and his involvement was crucial for unifying various rebel factions, especially in Delhi.

- **Response to British Provocation**: The British decision to exile Zafar and destroy the Mughal dynasty pushed him towards supporting the rebellion, as he saw it as a fight for survival and resistance to British rule.

- **Emotional Appeal**: The growing discontent among soldiers, peasants, and nobles in Delhi, coupled with the threat to the Mughal dynasty, prompted Zafar to bless the uprising in hopes of restoring the old order.

- **Desire for Restoration**: Zafar hoped to restore Mughal authority and control over India, which had been undermined by the British, leading him to lend his support to the 1857 rebellion

Ans – 7.) - **British Official Reports**: Accounts like the "Proceedings of the Government" and official British documents provided a colonial perspective on the revolt.

- **Rebel Proclamations**: Proclamations and writings from rebel leaders such as Bahadur Shah Zafar and Begum Hazrat Mahal highlight the goals and motivations of the insurgents.

- **Memoirs and Diaries**: Personal accounts from both British officials and Indian participants offer insights into the events and experiences of the revolt.

- **Newspapers and Magazines**: Publications from the time, including British and Indian newspapers, provide contemporary views and reactions to the rebellion.

- **Oral Traditions**: Oral narratives and folk songs passed down through generations help preserve the memory of the 1857 revolt, reflecting local perspectives.

- **Post-Revolt Histories**: Historians and scholars who wrote about the rebellion after its suppression provide analysis, though influenced by colonial or nationalist viewpoints

Ans – 8.)

- **Poems and Ballads**: Folk songs and poems were composed that celebrated Rani Lakshmi Bai's bravery and leadership during the revolt, making her a symbol of resistance.

- **Paintings**: Artists depicted her as a valiant queen, often showing her riding into battle, which became iconic representations of her courage and defiance.

- **Literary Works**: Writers like Subhadra Kumari Chauhan in Hindi literature immortalized Lakshmi Bai's role, portraying her as a heroic figure in the fight against British colonialism.

- **Nationalist Literature**: Post-revolt, literature romanticized her leadership, contributing to her status as a symbol of India's struggle for independence

Ans – 9.)

- **Military Action**: The British used superior military force, deploying reinforcements from other parts of the empire to suppress the revolt. For example, the British army recaptured Delhi after heavy fighting and restored British rule.

- **Siege and Brutality**: In key locations like Lucknow, Kanpur, and Jhansi, the British laid sieges, engaging in brutal reprisals against rebels, including executions and massacres.

- **Divide and Rule**: The British exploited divisions between different Indian communities, including using Hindu-Muslim divisions, to weaken the unity of the rebellion.

- **Use of Loyalists**: The British enlisted the help of loyal Indian rulers, such as the Nawab of Oudh and the Maharaja of Patiala, to fight against the rebels.

- **Repressive Measures**: Harsh laws were introduced to control public movements, and rebels were executed publicly to instill fear. For example, the British executed leaders like Mangal Pandey and Begum Hazrat Mahal's associates.

- **Establishment of Martial Law**: Martial law was enforced in many areas, with strict curfews and severe punishment for any suspected rebellion, curbing any chances of the uprising spreading

Ans – 10.)

- **Racial Discrimination**: Sepoys faced increasing racial discrimination, with British officers considering themselves superior to Indian soldiers, which led to resentment.

- **Pay and Benefits**: Sepoys were dissatisfied with the disparity in pay and allowances compared to their British counterparts, further straining their relationship with officers.

- **Harsh Discipline**: The imposition of harsh and demeaning discipline by British officers caused frustration and anger among sepoys, contributing to their alienation.

- **Cultural Insensitivity**: The British officers' disregard for Indian customs and beliefs, such as requiring sepoys to handle animal fats (pig and cow fat) in cartridges, heightened tensions.

- **Unfair Promotions**: British officers were often promoted based on race and connections, rather than merit, leading to a sense of injustice among sepoys who had been serving for long periods.

- **Loss of Respect**: As the British East India Company expanded, the sepoys' traditional role and respect gradually diminished, as they became more subject to foreign control and authority

Ans – 11.)

- **Lord Dalhousie's Statement (1851)**: Lord Dalhousie described Awadh as "a cherry that will drop into our mouth one day," hinting at its eventual annexation by the British.

- **Subsidiary Alliance (1801)**: The British imposed the Subsidiary Alliance on Awadh, requiring the Nawab to disband his military and allow British troops within his kingdom, making him increasingly dependent on British support.

- **Loss of Control**: As a result of the Subsidiary Alliance, the Nawab could no longer maintain control over rebellious chiefs and taluqdars within Awadh.

- **British Interests in Awadh**: The British were interested in Awadh's fertile soil for indigo and cotton cultivation, and its strategic location as a potential market for Upper India.

- **Territorial Annexation**: By the 1850s, most major regions of India had been annexed, and the British considered the annexation of Awadh as completing their territorial control over India.

- **Annexation of Awadh (1856)**: In 1856, Awadh was formally annexed to the British Empire, fulfilling the long-term British goal of territorial consolidation

Ans – 12.)

The **Subsidiary Alliance system** was introduced by **Lord Wellesley** in **1798** (not 1978), and it had the following provisions:

- **Stationing British Troops**: Indian rulers were required to maintain a British force within their territory, at their own expense, to protect them from external threats.

- **Non-Interference in Internal Affairs**: The rulers had to agree not to employ foreign mercenaries or make alliances without British approval.

- **Payment for British Troops**: The Indian ruler had to pay for the maintenance of British troops stationed in their kingdom, either in cash or land.

- **British Resident in the Court**: A British official (Resident) was to be stationed at the ruler's court to advise and ensure compliance with British interests.

- **Disbanding of Own Armies**: Rulers had to disband their own military forces or reduce them significantly, leaving them dependent on British military support.

- **Political and Military Control**: This system essentially gave the British control over the Indian state's foreign and military policies, leading to further British dominance in Indian affairs

Note – The Remaining questions are for your practice, hence their solutions aren't provided, Keep Practicing..!

Chapter – 11 (Mahatma Gandhi and the Nationalist Movement)

Ans – 1.)

- **Promoting National Unity**: Gandhi worked towards fostering unity among diverse communities, promoting harmony between Hindus and Muslims.

- **Economic Self-reliance**: He emphasized self-sufficiency through the Swadeshi Movement, encouraging the use of khadi and boycotting foreign goods.

- **Social Reforms**: Gandhi advocated for the abolition of untouchability and worked towards improving the status of Dalits, calling them Harijans.

- **Education and Rural Development**: He focused on basic education (Nai Talim) and the empowerment of rural India through community development programs.

- **Advocacy for Non-Violence**: Gandhi continued to promote his philosophy of non-violence (Ahimsa) in post-independence India, shaping the nation's social and political fabric.

- **Political Guidance**: He remained an influential leader, guiding the country through early challenges and promoting non-cooperation with the British even after independence

Ans – 2.) • **Autobiography**: Gandhi's *My Experiments with Truth* offers personal insights into his political philosophy and journey.

- **Speeches and Writings**: His speeches and articles, particularly in *Young India* and *Harijan*, provide a record of his thoughts on politics, society, and religion.

- **Letters**: Gandhi's extensive correspondence with leaders, followers, and the British government sheds light on his political strategies and personal views.

- **Biographies**: Several biographies, such as *Gandhi: A Life* by Yogesh Chandra and others, detail his political activities and leadership.

- **Newspapers and Journals**: Publications like *The Hindustan Times* and *The Times of India* provide contemporary accounts of his role in the nationalist movement.

- **Official Records**: British government documents and reports from the time also offer perspectives on Gandhi's influence on Indian politics.

* **Photographs and Documentaries**: Visual materials from his life help illustrate key events, movements, and interactions in the nationalist struggle.

Ans – 3.)

* **Widespread Participation**: The Salt Satyagraha (1930) mobilized millions across India, transcending regional, linguistic, and social divisions, making it one of the largest mass movements.

* **Symbol of Resistance**: Salt, an essential commodity, was heavily taxed by the British, making the protest against it a symbol of unjust colonial policies.

* **Mass Mobilization**: Gandhi's call for civil disobedience against the salt tax attracted not only Congress leaders but also common people, including peasants, women, and students.

* **Non-Violent Resistance**: The Salt Satyagraha emphasized non-violence (ahimsa) and non-cooperation, aligning with Gandhi's vision of peaceful resistance against British rule.

* **National Impact**: The movement spread rapidly across the country, leading to large-scale protests, boycotts of British goods, and the arrest of thousands, showing the strength of civil disobedience

Ans – 4.)

* **Widespread Participation**: The Non-Cooperation Movement (NCM) (1920-1922) saw participation from diverse sections of society, including peasants, workers, students, women, and the middle class, uniting them against British rule.

* **Boycotting British Goods**: People across India boycotted British goods, schools, courts, and services, which weakened the British administrative and economic structure.

* **Non-Violence and Non-Cooperation**: The movement was based on Gandhi's principle of non-violence, with peaceful protests, strikes, and picketing becoming widespread, ensuring mass involvement.

* **National Awakening**: The mass cooperation led to a collective sense of identity and unity among Indians, transcending regional and communal divides.

* **Mass Agitation**: The boycott of foreign goods, withdrawal from government institutions, and refusal to pay taxes were key forms of resistance, significantly undermining British authority

Ans – 5.)

- **Opposition to Untouchability**: Gandhi led the fight against untouchability, calling the untouchables "Harijans" (children of God), and worked towards their social inclusion.

- **Promotion of Khadi**: He advocated for the use of Khadi as a symbol of self-reliance and resistance to British economic exploitation.

- **Women's Empowerment**: Gandhi emphasized the importance of women's participation in the freedom movement and supported their education, social equality, and economic independence.

- **Education Reform**: Gandhi promoted basic education (Nai Talim) based on manual labor, aiming for self-sufficiency and character development.

- **Religious Tolerance**: He worked to bridge the gap between Hindus and Muslims, promoting communal harmony and tolerance across religious lines.

- **Fight for Social Justice**: Gandhi worked to alleviate poverty, improve the status of women, and promote a more equitable society

Ans – 6.)

- **Leadership**: Gandhi took the leadership of the Civil Disobedience Movement (CDM) after the failure of the Simon Commission and the lack of progress in the negotiations with the British government.

- **Salt March**: The 1930 Salt March, where Gandhi and his followers marched to Dandi to make salt in defiance of British laws, was a major catalyst for the movement.

- **Non-Violence**: Gandhi emphasized the principle of non-violence (ahimsa) throughout the CDM, urging followers to resist peacefully despite provocation.

- **Mass Participation**: The movement witnessed massive participation from all sections of society, including women, students, and the rural population, under Gandhi's leadership.

- **Boycott of British Goods**: Gandhi called for the boycott of British goods, institutions, and the British-imposed salt tax, leading to widespread non-cooperation.

- **Arrests and Repression**: Gandhi and many other leaders were arrested, but the movement continued to gain momentum as people took part in protests, strikes, and acts of civil disobedience.

- **Global Attention**: The movement garnered global attention, highlighting India's struggle for independence and putting pressure on the British government

Ans – 7.)

- **Leadership**: Gandhi ji emerged as the leader of the Non-Cooperation Movement (NCM) in 1920 after the Jallianwala Bagh massacre and the disillusionment with British rule.

- **Non-Violence**: Gandhi emphasized non-violence (ahimsa) as the central principle of the movement, urging peaceful resistance against British policies.

- **Boycott of British Goods**: He called for a complete boycott of British goods, institutions, and titles, promoting the use of swadeshi (Indian-made) products.

- **Non-Cooperation with British Institutions**: Gandhi encouraged Indians to resign from government services, boycott schools and colleges, and refuse to participate in elections.

- **Khadi Movement**: Gandhi promoted the spinning of khadi (handwoven cloth) as a symbol of self-reliance and opposition to British textiles.

- **Mass Participation**: The movement saw widespread participation from various sections of society, including students, women, and peasants, especially in rural areas.

- **Chauri Chaura Incident**: The movement was temporarily suspended in 1922 after the Chauri Chaura incident, where protesters killed policemen, violating Gandhi's principle of non-violence.

- **Impact**: Although the movement was halted, it marked a major shift in Indian politics and contributed to the growing sense of national unity and self-determination

Ans – 8.)

- **Nationwide Participation**: The Quit India Movement (1942) saw participation from people across India, including rural areas, cities, and all sections of society.

- **Mass Protests**: Widespread protests, strikes, and demonstrations took place in various regions, with people defying British authority on a large scale.

- **All-Inclusive Leadership**: Leaders from various political parties, including Congress, social groups, and workers, supported the movement, making it a broad-based national struggle.

- **Civil Disobedience**: Like earlier movements, it involved non-violent resistance, including picketing, boycotts, and refusal to cooperate with British authorities.

- **Women's Active Role**: Women actively participated in protests, further contributing to the mass nature of the movement.

• **Repression and Imprisonment**: The British responded with mass arrests and repression, imprisoning thousands, including key Congress leaders, which further galvanized public support.

• **Call for Immediate Independence**: The slogan "Do or Die" symbolized the urgency of the movement, appealing to people of all backgrounds for India's immediate freedom from British rule

Ans – 9.)

Reasons for the Salt Satyagraha:

• **Salt Tax**: The British imposed a heavy salt tax, which affected the poor and was seen as unjust by Indians, as salt was a basic necessity.

• **British Monopoly on Salt**: The British government controlled the production and sale of salt, preventing Indians from collecting it from natural sources like sea coasts.

• **Symbolic Protest**: Salt was a symbol of British exploitation and the movement aimed to challenge British authority over the most basic resources.

• **Gandhi's Strategy**: Gandhi used the salt tax as a way to unite people of all communities in a non-violent struggle against British rule.

Outcomes of this Satyagraha –

• **Widespread Participation**: The movement saw mass participation from people across India, including women, farmers, and urban workers

• **Nationwide Impact**: Gandhi's march to Dandi (1930) and the subsequent civil disobedience across the country made salt a focal point of protest.

• **International Attention**: The movement drew global attention to India's independence struggle and highlighted the injustices of British colonial rule.

• **Repression by the British**: The British responded with mass arrests, including the arrest of Gandhi, but this only strengthened the resolve of the Indian population.

• **Increased Nationalist Sentiment**: The success of the movement strengthened the Indian National Congress and created greater unity among Indians, setting the stage for larger struggles in the future.

• **British Concessions**: While the British did not immediately end the salt tax, the movement demonstrated the power of non-violent resistance and contributed to the broader Indian independence movement

Ans – 10.)

Causes of the Quit India Movement –

- **Failure of Cripps Mission (1942)**: The British government's proposal for Indian self-rule after World War II was rejected by the Indian National Congress, leading to a breakdown in negotiations.

- **Demand for Full Independence**: Gandhi and the Congress leadership believed that India should be granted complete independence, not just a limited self-rule, especially during the war.

- **Impact of World War II**: The war created economic hardships in India, leading to widespread discontent. People were affected by rising prices, shortages, and famine.

- **Japanese Threat**: The fear of Japanese expansion in Southeast Asia and their possible entry into India led the Congress to demand an immediate end to British rule to safeguard India's future.

- **Frustration with British Rule**: The long-standing demand for independence, the economic impact of British policies, and the failure of British reforms intensified the demand for immediate freedom

Events Happened in the Quit India movement –

- **Gandhi's Call for 'Do or Die'**: On August 8, 1942, at the Bombay session of the All India Congress Committee, Gandhi launched the Quit India Movement with the slogan "Do or Die" in the face of British colonial rule.

- **Immediate Repression**: The British arrested all Congress leaders, including Gandhi, Nehru, and Patel, which led to spontaneous protests and violence across the country.

- **Mass Participation**: People from all walks of life—students, workers, peasants, and leaders—joined the movement, despite the repression.

- **Protests and Strikes**: Nationwide strikes, protests, and demonstrations erupted, especially in cities like Bombay, Calcutta, and Lucknow. The movement also saw acts of sabotage and violence against British institutions.

- **Failure of the Movement**: Despite widespread participation, the movement was crushed by the British through arrests and military force, and the Congress was banned

- **Mass Repression**: Thousands were arrested, and many people were killed in police action. However, the movement left a lasting impression on the British government and Indian society.

- **Increased Nationalism**: Although it was suppressed, the movement demonstrated the unity and resolve of the Indian people for independence.

Ans - 11.) Answer would be same as Answer no. 4 and 7 (Mahatma Gandhi and the National movement)

Ans - 12.)

Reasons due to which Gandhiji choose salt for doing satyagraha are as follows □

- **Symbol of Oppression**: Salt was a basic necessity for all Indians, and the British monopoly on its production and sale was a symbol of colonial exploitation.

- **Widely Felt Grievance**: The salt tax affected everyone, regardless of class, caste, or religion, making it a unifying issue for people across India.

- **Non-Violent Protest**: Gandhi believed that the salt tax was an issue that could be addressed through non-violent means, aligning with his philosophy of satyagraha.

- **Challenge to British Authority**: By defying the salt laws, Gandhi aimed to directly challenge British colonial authority and show the power of peaceful resistance.

- **Universal Impact**: Salt was consumed by all sections of society, from the poor to the rich, and the tax on it was seen as an unjust burden.

- **Accessible Protest**: Salt was readily available in many parts of India, making it easy for people from rural and urban areas to participate in the protest

Becoming an All India Campaign:

- **Salt March (1930)**: Gandhi's 240-mile Salt March from Sabarmati to Dandi in Gujarat was the starting point, where he made salt from the sea, defying British laws.

- **Mass Participation**: Gandhi's call for non-violent resistance spread quickly across the country, with many joining the movement by making their own salt or protesting salt taxes.

- **National Unity**: The salt satyagraha transcended regional, religious, and caste divisions, bringing people from all walks of life together in a unified struggle for independence.

- **Widespread Impact**: The campaign spread across India, with people in different regions participating in salt-making, protests, and boycotting British goods, making it a mass movement

Ans – 13.)

- **Salt March (1930)**: Gandhi led the Salt March, a significant act of defiance against British salt laws, symbolizing non-violent resistance.

- **Civil Disobedience Movement (1930-34)**: Following the Salt March, Gandhi launched the Civil Disobedience Movement, urging Indians to refuse cooperation with British laws, especially the salt tax.

- **Nationwide Protests**: The movement spread across India, with mass participation in making salt, boycotting British goods, and picketing liquor shops.

- **Imprisonment**: Gandhi was arrested in 1930, along with thousands of followers, and was later released in 1931 after the Gandhi-Irwin Pact.

- **Gandhi-Irwin Pact (1931)**: Gandhi negotiated with Lord Irwin, leading to the suspension of the Civil Disobedience Movement and the release of political prisoners.

- **Round Table Conferences (1930-32)**: Gandhi attended the Second Round Table Conference in London in 1931 to discuss constitutional reforms, but no significant progress was made.

- **Re-launch of Civil Disobedience (1932)**: After the failure of the Second Round Table Conference, Gandhi re-launched the movement in 1932, leading to further arrests.

- **Famine Relief Work (1932)**: Gandhi focused on famine relief during the widespread famine in India, highlighting the urgency of economic reforms.

- **Focus on Social Issues**: Gandhi continued his campaign against untouchability and worked on spreading the message of "Harijan" (children of God), advocating for the upliftment of lower castes.

- **1934 Resignation**: Gandhi resigned from the Congress Working Committee in 1934, deciding to focus on rural development and social reforms

Ans – 14.)
- **Non-Violent Resistance**: Gandhi emphasized non-violence (ahimsa) as the central principle of the Indian struggle for independence, marking a shift from violent resistance.

- **Non-Cooperation Movement (1920-22)**: He launched the Non-Cooperation Movement, urging Indians to boycott British goods, services, and educational institutions, encouraging self-reliance.

- **Mass Mobilization**: Gandhi expanded the base of the freedom struggle by involving people from all sections of society, including peasants, workers, and women.

- **Khadi Movement**: He promoted the use of khadi (handwoven cloth) as a symbol of self-reliance, reducing dependence on British textiles.

- **Satyagraha**: Gandhi introduced satyagraha (truth-force) as a method of non-violent protest, exemplified in campaigns like the Champaran and Kheda struggles.

- **Cultural and Social Revival**: Gandhi's emphasis on simplicity, self-reliance, and social reform fostered a sense of unity and pride in Indian culture, distancing Indians from colonial influences.

- **Leadership Style**: Gandhi's personal example of leading a simple, austere life made him a symbol of moral authority, contrasting with the British colonial rulers.

- **Focus on Rural India**: Gandhi focused on rural issues like land reforms, peasant rights, and improving the condition of untouchables, making the movement relevant to the masses.

- **End of Moderate Politics**: Gandhi's rise marked the end of the moderate phase of the Congress, shifting the movement towards more direct and radical forms of protest.

- **Impact on National Unity**: His methods united diverse sections of society, laying the foundation for a pan-Indian nationalist movement that transcended regional and communal differences

Ans – 15.) Answer would be same as Answer no, 9 and 12 (Mahatma Gandhi and National Movement)

Ans – 16.) **Strengths –**

- **Autobiography**: Gandhi's autobiography provides a direct insight into his thoughts, motivations, and personal experiences.

- **Writings and Speeches**: His numerous speeches and writings offer valuable perspectives on his ideologies, strategies, and vision for India's independence.

- **Letters and Correspondence**: Gandhi's letters to political leaders, followers, and the British authorities help understand his political tactics and responses to events.

- **Official Records**: British colonial documents and reports give a perspective on how Gandhi's actions were viewed by the colonial government.

- **Contemporary Accounts**: Newspapers and journals from the time document public opinion, providing external viewpoints on Gandhi's leadership and activities.

- **Memoirs of Followers**: Writings of his close associates and followers give a first-hand account of Gandhi's leadership style and activities.

Limitations –

- **Bias in Colonial Sources**: British records often portrayed Gandhi in a negative light, reflecting colonial bias.

- **Limited Accounts from Opponents**: Sources from political rivals or dissenters are scarce, limiting a comprehensive understanding of the opposition to Gandhi's ideas.

- **Incomplete Documentation**: Some of Gandhi's actions, especially in the early phases, were not well-documented or preserved.

- **Self-Censorship**: Gandhi's own writings sometimes omit or gloss over aspects of his political career that were controversial or personally difficult.

- **Interpretations Vary**: Different interpretations of Gandhi's actions and legacy may lead to conflicting portrayals in historical accounts.

- **Subjectivity in Biographies**: Biographies and personal accounts often reflect the perspectives and biases of the authors

Ans – 17.) • **Economic Hardship**: The country was facing widespread poverty, famine, and economic distress, especially in rural areas.

- **Colonial Exploitation**: British colonial policies were draining India's resources, leading to a growing sense of economic exploitation.

- **Growing Nationalist Movement**: The Indian National Congress (INC) had become more politically active, with increasing calls for self-rule.

- **Rise of Social Reforms**: Social reform movements, particularly in areas like education and the abolition of untouchability, were gaining momentum.

- **World War I Impact**: The First World War (1914-1918) had begun, leading to political unrest and a demand for constitutional reforms from the British government.

- **Division Between Communities**: Tensions between different communities, particularly Hindus and Muslims, were becoming more pronounced

Chapter -12 (Framing the Constitution)

Ans – 1.)

- **Opposition to Separate Electorates**: Nationalists strongly opposed the idea of separate electorates after partition, fearing it would deepen divisions within the country.

- **Fear of Ongoing Conflict**: There was a deep concern that separate electorates would lead to continued civil war, riots, and violence, further fragmenting the nation.

- **Patel's Warning**: Sardar Patel described separate electorates as a "poison" that had infected the political body of the country, highlighting its destructive impact.

- **Divisiveness**: The demand for separate electorates had caused communities to turn against each other, exacerbating the divide between them and fostering a climate of hostility.

- **Impact on National Unity**: Separate electorates had not only divided the nation but also led to bloodshed, contributing to the tragic partition of India.

- **Patel's Call for Peace**: Patel urged for the abolition of separate electorates, emphasizing that only through unity could peace be restored in the country.

Ans – 2.)

- **Unity and Integrity**: Some members of the Constituent Assembly argued for a strong central government to maintain the unity and integrity of the newly independent nation, which was divided by regional, cultural, and linguistic differences.

- **Preventing Fragmentation**: The experience of partition and the potential for regional conflicts led many to believe that a strong centre was necessary to prevent the country from fragmenting.

- **Economic Stability**: A strong central government was seen as essential for ensuring economic stability and uniform development across all regions, especially after the destruction caused by partition.

- **National Defense**: A powerful central government was considered crucial for ensuring national defense and security, especially in the context of potential external threats and internal unrest.

- **Consistency in Law and Policy**: A strong centre was believed to be important for ensuring consistency in laws, policies, and governance across the country, preventing disparities between states.

- **Handling Communal Tensions**: In the aftermath of partition and ongoing communal tensions, a strong central authority was viewed as necessary to prevent violence and maintain law and order.

- **Consolidating National Identity**: The members believed a strong central government could help in consolidating a national identity and overcoming regional and linguistic diversities

Ans – 3.)

- **Constituent Assembly Composition**: The Constituent Assembly had 300 members, with six playing particularly important roles in shaping the Indian Constitution.

- **Congress Trio**: Three Congress leaders were pivotal: Jawaharlal Nehru, Vallabhbhai Patel, and Rajendra Prasad.

- **Nehru's Role**: Nehru moved the crucial "Objectives Resolution" and proposed the design of India's National Flag, a horizontal tricolour with saffron, white, and green, featuring a navy blue wheel.

- **Patel's Contribution**: Patel worked behind the scenes, playing a key role in drafting several reports and reconciling opposing viewpoints.

- **Rajendra Prasad's Role**: Rajendra Prasad, as President of the Assembly, steered discussions, ensuring all members had the opportunity to contribute.

- **B.R. Ambedkar's Leadership**: B.R. Ambedkar, the lawyer and economist, was appointed as the law minister and served as Chairman of the Drafting Committee of the Constitution.

- **Key Legal Advisors**: K.M. Munshi from Gujarat and Alladi Krishnaswamy Aiyar from Madras provided crucial inputs during the drafting process.

- **B.N. Rau's Contribution**: B.N. Rau, the Constitutional Advisor, assisted the committee by preparing background papers and studying political systems in other countries for reference

Ans – 4.)

- **Three Lists in Federalism**: The draft constitution of India provided for three lists of subjects to define the distribution of powers between the central and state governments.

- **Union List**: The Union List included subjects on which only the central government could legislate. Example: Defence, foreign affairs, and atomic energy.

- **State List**: The State List included subjects on which only state governments could legislate. Example: Police, public health, and local government.

- **Concurrent List**: The Concurrent List contained subjects on which both the central and state governments could legislate. Example: Education, marriage, and criminal law.

- **Importance of the Three Lists**: These lists helped maintain a balance of power between the central and state governments, while also allowing for flexibility in governance.

- **Central Override**: In case of conflict between central and state laws on a concurrent subject, the central law would prevail. Example: The central government passed laws on education, but states could also enact laws as long as they did not conflict.

Ans – 5.)

- **Govind Ballabh Pant's Opposition**: Pant opposed the demand for separate electorates, arguing it was harmful for both the nation and minorities.

- **Democracy's Success**: Pant agreed with Bahadur that a successful democracy should build confidence among all sections of society.

- **Rights and Respect**: Every citizen should be treated in a way that satisfies both their material needs and spiritual sense of self-respect.

- **Majority's Obligation**: The majority community had an obligation to understand the problems of minorities and empathize with their aspirations.

- **Danger of Separate Electorates**: Pant called the demand for separate electorates "suicidal," arguing it would isolate minorities and deprive them of influence within the government.

- **Loyalty to the State**: While cultural rights could be granted, all citizens should offer loyalty to the State and act as equal members, avoiding divided loyalties.

- **Citizen vs. Community**: Pant emphasized that the focus should be on citizens, not communities, stating that the citizen forms the foundation and peak of the social pyramid.

- **Fear of Divided Loyalties**: Despite recognizing community rights, nationalists feared that focusing too much on communities could weaken the unity of the nation and the strength of the State.

Ans – 6.)

- **Central vs. State Powers Debate**: A major issue discussed in the Constituent Assembly was the division of powers between the central and state governments.

- **Need for Strong Centre**: Some members argued for a strong central government to ensure unity and prevent disintegration of the country, especially given the diversity of regions, languages, and cultures.

- **Fear of Fragmentation**: Concerns were raised that too much power to states could lead to fragmentation, as different regions might have conflicting interests, threatening national integrity.

- **Federal Structure**: The framers of the Constitution adopted a federal structure, where certain powers were allocated to the central government, while others were reserved for states, as outlined in the Union, State, and Concurrent lists.

- **Central Government's Role**: Supporters of a strong central government emphasized the need for uniform policies and central control over critical areas like defense, foreign relations, and national security.

- **State Autonomy**: On the other hand, proponents of state autonomy stressed the importance of local governance and the need for states to have control over areas like education, health, and agriculture to address local needs.

- **Resolution through Union List**: The final structure of the Constitution included a clear demarcation of powers, with the Union List giving exclusive powers to the central government and the State List reserving powers for the states.

- **Balancing Interests**: The Concurrent List, where both central and state governments could legislate, was included to balance the need for central authority with state interests, particularly in areas of shared concern.

- **Emergency Provisions**: The Constitution also included provisions for a strong central government during times of national emergency, further reinforcing central control in exceptional circumstances.

- **Legacy of the Debate**: This debate on the balance of power has shaped the ongoing relationship between central and state governments, with periodic discussions about the distribution of powers and state autonomy

Ans – 7.)

- **Objective Resolution**: The Objective Resolution was a resolution moved by Jawaharlal Nehru in the Constituent Assembly on December 13, 1946.

- **Purpose**: It outlined the fundamental principles on which the Constitution of India would be based, expressing the aspirations and values of the newly independent nation.

- **Key Provisions**: It emphasized India as a sovereign, democratic, and republic state, where all people, regardless of religion, race, or caste, would have equal rights and opportunities.

- **Role in Constitution**: It called for the adoption of a Constitution that would guarantee fundamental rights, ensure justice, and safeguard the unity and integrity of India.

- **Vision for Future**: The resolution also emphasized social, economic, and political justice, ensuring the welfare of all citizens and equality before the law.

- **Momentous Nature**: The resolution is considered momentous because it laid the foundational philosophy for the Indian Constitution and set the direction for the drafting of the Constitution.

- **Symbol of Unity**: It represented the collective vision of India's leaders and a clear commitment to democratic governance, social justice, and secularism.

- **Inspiration for Constitution**: The resolution was later incorporated into the preamble of the Indian Constitution, marking its significance in shaping the nation's legal framework.

- **A Defining Moment**: The passing of this resolution was a turning point in India's constitutional history, as it signified the formal and collective resolve of the country's leaders to establish a democratic republic.

- **Historical Importance**: It marked the beginning of the process of drafting the Indian Constitution and is regarded as one of the key moments in India's transition from colonial rule to independence

Ans – 8.)

- **National Unity**: A strong central government was seen as crucial for maintaining national unity, particularly in a newly independent country with diverse languages, cultures, and religions.

- **Avoiding Fragmentation**: It was feared that weak central authority could lead to fragmentation of the nation, with states pursuing their own interests at the expense of national cohesion.

- **Coordinating Policies**: A strong centre would ensure uniform policies and laws across the country, preventing regional disparities and promoting balanced development.

- **Security and Defense**: National security, including defense against external threats and maintaining law and order, could be more effectively managed by a strong central government.

- **Economic Integration**: A strong centre would be able to integrate the economy and ensure coordination between various states for economic development and resource management.

- **Protection of Minorities**: A strong central government was seen as necessary to protect the interests of minorities and ensure their rights were safeguarded across all regions.

- **Crisis Management**: A central authority could respond quickly and decisively in times of national emergencies, ensuring timely intervention and resolution of crises.

- **Consistency in Governance**: A strong centre would promote consistent governance and the rule of law, reducing the chances of political instability or conflicting state-level policies.

- **Preserving Constitutional Framework**: A strong central government was seen as necessary to preserve the constitutional framework and ensure the implementation of constitutional mandates across the country.

- **Ambedkar's Stand**: Dr. B.R. Ambedkar called for a strong and united Centre, stronger than the one created under the Government of India Act of 1935.

- **Security Concerns**: Given the widespread communal riots and violence, members argued that a strong central government was necessary to manage and control the situation.

- **Gopalaswami Ayyangar's View**: Ayyangar stressed that the Centre should be made as strong as possible to ensure national stability and unity.

- **Balakrishna Sharma's Argument**: Sharma argued that only a strong Centre could plan for the country's welfare, mobilize economic resources, establish a proper administration, and defend the nation from foreign threats

Ans – 9.) • **Linguistic Diversity in India**: India's vast linguistic diversity was a major concern during the drafting of the Constitution. There were debates over how to address the issue of language in a unified country.

- **Language as Identity**: Language was viewed as a key factor of identity for various communities, and members of the Constituent Assembly recognized the need to preserve regional languages and cultures.

- **Official Language Debate**: A major issue was whether Hindi should be the sole national language or if other languages should be given official status.

- **Role of Regional Languages**: Several members, especially from non-Hindi speaking regions, advocated for the recognition of their regional languages, fearing the marginalization of their linguistic heritage.

- **Provision for Bilingualism**: The debate led to a compromise with the provision that both Hindi and English would be used for official purposes for a period of 15 years after independence.

- **Language of Education**: There was a significant discussion on the medium of instruction in schools and universities, with a strong push to include regional languages in educational systems to make education more accessible.

- **State Reorganization**: Linguistic issues were also linked to the reorganization of states. The demand for states based on linguistic lines, such as the creation of Andhra Pradesh in 1953, arose from the need to address linguistic identity in governance.

- **Constitutional Provisions**: The Constitution eventually recognized 22 languages under the Eighth Schedule, and these languages were granted equal status as official languages in respective states.

Ans – 10.)

Opponents of Separate Electorate –

- **Congress Leaders (Jawaharlal Nehru, Mahatma Gandhi, Sardar Patel)**:

  - **Argument**: Congress opposed separate electorates, believing they would divide the Indian nation along religious lines, perpetuate communal divisions, and weaken the unity of India. They argued that all communities should have equal rights and that shared electorates would foster national integration.

- **Sardar Vallabhbhai Patel**:

  - **Argument**: Patel argued that separate electorates were detrimental to national unity and would isolate communities, leading to further fragmentation. He stressed that all citizens should be treated equally within one national framework, not as members of separate religious or social groups.

- **Mahatma Gandhi**:

  - **Argument**: Gandhi vehemently opposed separate electorates, believing that it would make communities distrustful and lead to permanent divisions. He advocated for a common electorate where people of all religions could come together, emphasizing Hindu-Muslim unity.

- **Govind Ballabh Pant**:

    - **Argument**: Pant argued that separate electorates would permanently isolate minorities, depriving them of effective participation in the mainstream political process, and would lead to divided loyalties within the nation.

Supporters of Separate Electorate –

- **B. Pocker Bahadur**

- On 27 August 1947, B. Pocker Bahadur from Madras advocated for the continuation of separate electorates for minorities.

- He argued that minorities exist in all countries and could not be eliminated or ignored.

- Bahadur believed that to ensure harmony between communities, there must be a political framework where minorities are well represented.

- He emphasized that separate electorates were essential for giving minorities, particularly Muslims, a meaningful voice in governance.

- According to Bahadur, non-Muslims could not fully understand the needs of Muslims, nor could they choose a true representative for the Muslim community.

- He asserted that separate electorates would allow Muslims to have their interests properly addressed in the political system.

Ans – 11.)

- Balakrishna Sharma argued that a strong Centre was necessary for the well-being of the entire country.

- He believed that only a powerful central government could mobilize economic resources effectively.

- He emphasized that the Centre should plan and coordinate national development.

- Sharma highlighted that a strong Centre was essential to maintain proper administration across the country.

- He argued that the Centre was crucial for defending the nation against foreign aggression.

• Sharma suggested that a strong Centre would help in managing communal tensions and violence effectively.

Ans – 12.)

• **Demand for Separate Electorates**: Ambedkar had initially demanded separate electorates for the Depressed Castes, but Gandhi opposed this, arguing it would permanently segregate them from society.

• **Constitutional Resolution**: The Constituent Assembly sought a middle ground by ensuring protections for the Depressed Castes without separate electorates, aiming for their integration into society.

• **Protection and Safeguards**: The Assembly decided to abolish untouchability, open Hindu temples to all castes, and reserve seats in legislatures and jobs in government for the Depressed Castes.

• **Numerical Strength**: Members like J. Nagappa highlighted that the Depressed Castes were not a minority, as they constituted 20-25% of the population, but were marginalized due to social norms.

• **Social Marginalization**: The Depressed Castes were denied access to education, administration, and social interaction, facing widespread discrimination and exclusion.

• **Need for Attitudinal Change**: It was recognized that legal protections alone would not suffice to end discrimination; a societal shift in attitudes towards the Depressed Castes was also necessary.

• **End of Separate Electorates**: After the Partition, Ambedkar no longer advocated for separate electorates, accepting the constitutional measures that focused on integration and equality.

• **Measures Welcomed**: The provisions made in the Constitution were welcomed as a step towards equality, though there was recognition that complete social change would take time

Ans – 13.)

• **Representation of Public Interests**: The Constituent Assembly aimed to represent the diverse sections of Indian society, and its discussions were influenced by public sentiments and concerns.

• **Debates on Minority Rights**: The Assembly considered public opinions about the rights and protections of minorities, especially religious and caste-based minorities, when discussing issues

• **Role of Press and Media**: The press played a crucial role in shaping public opinions on constitutional matters, and these views were reflected in the Assembly debates, influencing key decisions.

- **Social Movements and Leaders**: The influence of social movements, such as those advocating for the rights of the Depressed Castes, and leaders like Gandhi and Ambedkar, shaped the discussions and decisions in the Assembly.

- **Public Agitation and Protests**: Widespread public agitations and protests, especially after events like the Partition, impacted the Assembly's decisions on issues like minority protection, language, and federalism.

- **Public Sentiment on Governance**: Public opinion on governance models, such as the demand for a strong central government, influenced debates on the distribution of powers between the Centre and the States.

- **Feedback from Provincial Assemblies**: The views and concerns of provincial assemblies and regional representatives also helped shape discussions in the Constituent Assembly, ensuring the representation of local public opinions.

- **Social and Economic Expectations**: The aspirations of the masses, particularly for social justice, economic equality, and the abolition of untouchability, influenced the Assembly's approach to these issues in the Constitution.

- **Pressure from Political Parties**: Political parties, which represented different sections of society, often voiced the concerns and desires of their constituencies, influencing the debates in the Assembly.

- **Inclusion of Public Input**: Public consultations and the involvement of experts and civil society groups ensured that the Constitution reflected the aspirations and values of the Indian populace

Ans – 14.) • **Somnath Lahiri's Concern**: Communist member Somnath Lahiri believed that British imperialism still influenced the proceedings of the Constituent Assembly.

- **Call for Independence**: Lahiri urged both the members and the general public to completely break free from the lingering effects of British rule.

- **Context of the Deliberations**: The Assembly's deliberations took place in late 1946-47, while the British were still present in India.

- **British Influence**: Despite the Indian administration under Jawaharlal Nehru, it was still operating under the guidance of the Viceroy and the British Government in London.

- **Lahiri's Criticism**: He pointed out that the Constituent Assembly, being British-made, was still implementing British plans, as per the interests of the British authorities

Note – The Remaining questions are for your practice, hence their solutions aren't provided

Thank You!

Dear Reader,

Thank you for choosing **History MasterGuide** as your academic companion. This book has been meticulously crafted to provide comprehensive support for Class XII students navigating the fascinating journey of history.

Your trust in this resource means the world to us, and we are committed to helping you achieve your academic goals with clarity and confidence.

Your Feedback Matters

This guide is a reflection of our dedication to students like you, and your feedback helps us improve. If you have any suggestions or questions, feel free to reach out.

- Email us at: discof2007vedant@gmail.com

- Follow us for updates and tips: EducatorVedant (Telegram ID)

Thank you for letting **History MasterGuide** be a part of your academic success story.

Wishing you all the best in your studies and beyond!

Warm regards,
Vedant Gupta
Author, Educator, and History Enthusiast